Cooking
for Isaiah

Cooking
for Isaiah

Gluten-Free & Dairy-Free
Recipes for Easy, Delicious Meals

Silvana Nardone

PHOTOGRAPHS BY STEPHEN SCOTT GROSS

The Reader's Digest Association, Inc.
New York • Montreal

First printing in paperback 2012

Project Editor: Andrea Chesman
Copy Editor: Barbara Booth
Interior Design: Vertigo Design NYC
Cover Designer: George McKeon
Consulting Art Director: Elizabeth Tunnicliffe
Food Stylist: Tracey Seaman
Prop Stylist: Meghan Guthrie
Indexer: Nan Badgett

TRADE PUBLISHING
Senior Art Director: George McKeon
Executive Editor: Dolores York
Manufacturing Manager: Elizabeth Dinda
Associate Publisher: Rosanne McManus
President and Publisher: Harold Clarke

THE READER'S DIGEST ASSOCIATION, INC.
President and Chief Executive Officer: Robert E. Guth
President, North America: Dan Lagani

ISBN 978-1-60652-165-6 (hardcover)
ISBN 978-1-60652-565-4 (paperback)

Library of Congress Cataloging-in-Publication Data
Nardone, Silvana.
 Cooking for Isaiah : gluten-free & dairy-free recipes for easy, delicious meals / Silvana Nardone.
    p. cm.
 Includes index.
 ISBN 978-1-60652-165-6
 1. Gluten-free diet--Recipes. 2. Milk-free diet--Recipes. I. Reader's Digest Association. II. Title.
 RM237.86.N37 2010
 641.5'638--dc22
                        2010014371

For more products and information, visit our website:
    www.rd.com (in the United States)
    www.readersdigest.ca (in Canada)

Printed in China

1 3 5 7 9 10 8 6 4 2

To my angel Isaiah, my handsome son. You are the reason this cookbook exists—a delicious reminder that together, love and food are nature's greatest healer.

contents

foreword

I FELL IN LOVE WITH SILVANA FOR TWO REASONS: Number 1, her biscotti, and Number 2, her fig-and-rosemary wine crackers. The truth is that I never would've imagined Sil cooking without flour, because when I first met her five years ago, she owned an Italian bakery in Brooklyn. *Cooking for Isaiah* proves that she's an inspired, masterful baker and cook—with or without gluten and dairy. I can tell you firsthand, Silvana's food boggles my taste buds!

Sil always talks about her kids (as all mothers do), and we flip through beautiful pictures of Isaiah and Chiara whenever she's carrying around a new batch. One day she mentioned that Isaiah had to cut gluten and dairy from his diet. I wasn't sure what she was going to do, since she's such a bread- and cookie-baking mama, but leave it to Sil to get her kid fed! Some mothers would have looked up recipes, but she wrote them.

Every time we eat at Sil's house, we enjoy handmade pastas and fresh-from-the-oven desserts. A few of my favorite recipes are the Banana Pancakes with Warm Cinnamon Goo (page 26), Sloppy Joe–Stuffed Potato Skins (page 64), Pumpkin Dumplings with Bacon and Radicchio (page 104) and, of course, the Chocolate Birthday Cake with Whipped Chocolate Frosting (page 207)—after all, what's a birthday without the cake?

All the recipes in *Cooking for Isaiah* were written with love, and whether or not you need to limit gluten or dairy, you can taste that in every bite.

Love,

Rachael Ray

introduction

I AM NOT A DOCTOR. I AM NOT A NUTRITIONIST. I AM NOT A TRAINED CHEF. I AM NOT A FOOD SCIENTIST. I AM JUST A MOM WHO WANTS TO FEED HER KIDS. And hunger does not wait. Like a good Italian-American, I like to feed people. Even more, I like to make good food for people who love to eat—food that tastes like home. So when my 13-year-old son, Isaiah, was diagnosed with food sensitivities—to gluten and dairy—I wasn't going to let that turn our lives upside down.

But I couldn't imagine what life would be like in a gluten-free world. Let alone dairy-free or anything else-free. The one thing I knew for sure was that making good food was all about trial and error until I get to that something that I fall in love with and can't get enough of. I know it's really good when I crave it the next day and the memory of it lingers past the crumbs left on my lips. I could learn a new way to cook—and I would have to. I would heal Isaiah through a plate of pancakes. It was the only way I knew how.

Gone were the days when I could pick up Isaiah from school and stop at an Italian bakery for an afternoon snack. He'd stare endlessly into the big, shiny display case filled with rows and rows of sprinkle-coated cookies and pick out four or five. Memories flooded my head—a cup of hot chocolate, Isaiah's backpack hanging off his shoulder, a slice of pepperoni pizza, basketball shoes in the middle of our living room, ice cream before dinner. These were the daily rhythms of our lives. I struggled to cling to the smallest of details to keep them from slipping away. Overnight Isaiah had to cut out everything containing gluten and dairy.

Months earlier, Isaiah had developed warts all over his hands and knees. Friends reassured my husband, Stephen, and me that boys get warts and that they'd go away on their own. But watching him pull at his long-sleeve T-shirts to cover them up was heartbreaking. So we decided to take him to our pediatrician, who recommended an over-the-counter medication to remove them, but there were just too many warts. Then we took him to a dermatologist, who started to freeze them off, one by one, while Isaiah sat there gripping my hands and swallowing the pain. I asked the doctor to please stop. I can still see the scars on his knees.

But something the dermatologist had said kept ringing through my head: Warts are caused by a virus, and Isaiah's immune system should be able to fight them off. I wasn't sure what this meant, exactly. Searching for answers, I found myself e-mailing someone I had stumbled across on the Web—a homeopath—to ask for help. A few days later the homeopath prescribed immune-boosting supplements for Isaiah, but a month later nothing had changed. Then she ran a food-allergy test, and two weeks later we had our answers. Isaiah was intolerant to gluten and dairy. The homeopath turned to Isaiah and said, "You're lucky your mom is who she is."

Isaiah turned to me and asked, "What am I going to eat?"

Everything stopped. "What do you want to eat?" I asked.

"Cornbread."

Later that day, when we got home, I headed straight to the kitchen and started reading every label in the pantry, fridge and freezer. I cleaned out everything—breads, cheeses, cookies, ice cream, snack bars, cereals, condiments and candy. I didn't want Isaiah to see anything he couldn't eat. And there it was, all in one big pile: breakfast, lunch, snack and dinner as Isaiah had understood it for practically his whole life.

That Halloween, Isaiah dressed up as a vampire goblin. His then-one-year-old sister, Chiara, wore a fluffy dog costume and spent most of her evening riding around on her dad's shoulders. The next day, after Isaiah had shoved in as much

Halloween candy as he could stomach, he went gluten-free and dairy-free. Less than a month later, I cooked my first gluten-free and dairy-free Thanksgiving.

Then, early one winter morning, Isaiah woke up and ran into the kitchen screaming, "They're gone! Look, Mommy, the warts are gone!" I couldn't believe my eyes—poof, gone? In just two months Isaiah's body had quietly healed itself. That's when I knew that I had to mainstream our lives, which meant getting breakfast, lunch and dinner on the table—gluten-free and all. I didn't want to cook separate meals for different family members, so I needed recipes that worked for everybody every day.

I just wanted my family to be happy. I was desperate to blur the lines between gluten-free and gluten-full. I didn't want Isaiah to long for anything. Even more, I wanted him to forget. If I could only get him to stop thinking he was eating something gluten-free or dairy-free and start thinking how much he loved the food, then I would have accomplished what I had set out to do. I wanted Isaiah to experience firsthand that removing gluten from a recipe could mean that food could taste and look just as good, if not better, than its conventional counterpart.

The truth is, in the beginning, I knew nothing about cooking or baking without gluten or dairy. Almost every day, I found lunches piled away in Isaiah's room— stacks of plastic food containers with molded-over chili or snack bags with ham-and-cheese roll-ups. Junk-food wrappers lined his jeans pockets and littered his desk drawers. I had to do better. I had to work harder. Words like "creamy" and "crispy" and "chewy" more or less evaporated from our vocabulary.

I had to make Isaiah that cornbread, and it had to look and taste like cornbread. First, I had to find a substitute for gluten-full flour. I quickly realized that baking without gluten wasn't as simple as swapping flours. What could help the gluten-free flour behave the way I needed it to? I tasted, smelled and experimented with gluten-free flour after gluten-free flour, jotting down notes about likes and dislikes, successes and failures.

I started to play around with cornmeal-to-flour proportions, quantity of wet to dry ingredients, and on and on, in the hopes of getting the right texture, browning and flavor. The first cornbread I sliced crumbled into what seemed like a million little pieces and had an unappealing beanlike flavor, which came, predictably, from the chickpea-based, gluten-free flour blend I had used for the recipe. The second one I made held together nicely, but it was chalky and tasteless. The third was a wonder: The cornbread was flavorful, moist and light, with a deliciously tender crumb. My only hope with this recipe was that Isaiah would love it. Yes, that's true for everything I make, but none more than this. And then Isaiah took a bite. The look on his face was pure heaven.

My next task was to find a milk stand-in. I purchased every option available, and after I had lined them all up on our kitchen counter, we had a dizzying assortment of nut, rice, oat and hemp milks in front of us. We sipped them one by one, noting each flavor and consistency until we were convinced that what we tasted was unquestionably chocolate milk—a small, everlasting miracle stumbled upon in a sea of nondairy milk. Really, it was chocolate rice milk, and plain rice milk, though watery compared to cow's milk, became our everyday milk.

Then I was ready to rebuild our favorite recipes. Gradually I developed new ones that would deliver on taste and texture. It took some time, but eventually it all came together. I figured out how to make food that everyone can sit down and enjoy together. It's nice, after all, to live in a home where the fridge is always full. Isaiah is home again. Right where he belongs.

I hope you'll join us in the kitchen—and at our family table—one recipe at a time.

the basics

COOKING AND BAKING GLUTEN-FREE OR DAIRY-FREE IS EASIER THAN YOU THINK.
The trick is to choose ingredients not just for flavor, but for performance, so that cake is light and moist, pizza crust is tender and crisp, and gravy is rich and creamy. Besides gluten-free flours and rice milk, I use ingredients that you probably already have on hand.

In my recipes I reconstruct classic foods, so I'm looking for ingredients that deliver the same flavor principles. For instance, I was having trouble with my brownies (page 201). Batch after batch, Isaiah and I kept tasting something off, something that tasted almost like baking soda, but there was no baking soda in the recipe. It took a while to pinpoint the source of the off flavor, but ultimately we sniffed it out—it turned out to be the tapioca flour (also called tapioca starch) in my flour blend. So I went to the store and bought four different brands of tapioca flour. When I got home, I cut each one open and smelled inside. There was only one that had no noticeable scent: the tapioca flour from Shiloh Farms. I mixed up a new flour blend and baked off a batch of brownies—they tasted exactly right.

Before I started making my own all-purpose flour blend, I tried my share of store-bought ones. They were convenient, but expensive, and the package sizes were barely enough to make a batch of cookies. Another drawback was the types of flours used in the blends. Some contained buckwheat flour or bean flours, which didn't deliver that classic flavor or appearance I wanted.

Silvana's all-purpose flour blend

MAKES about 4 pounds **PREP TIME** 15 minutes

6 cups white rice flour, preferably Bob's Red Mill

3 cups tapioca flour, preferably Shiloh Farms

1½ cups potato starch, preferably Bob's Red Mill

1 tablespoon salt

2 tablespoons xanthan gum, preferably Bob's Red Mill

In a large bowl, whisk together the rice flour, tapioca flour, potato starch, salt and xanthan gum. Transfer to an airtight storage container and store in a cool, dry place or in the refrigerator.

Silvana's pancake mix

MAKES about 2½ pounds **PREP TIME** 8 minutes

9 cups Silvana's All-Purpose Flour Blend (above)

1 cup plus 2 tablespoons sugar

3 tablespoons baking powder

2¼ teaspoons salt

In a large bowl, whisk together the flour, sugar, baking powder and salt. Transfer to an airtight storage container and store in a cool, dry place or in the refrigerator.

Silvana's Pancake Mix

So I developed my own flour blend. I wanted it to have a limited number of ingredients and a neutral flavor so that I could use my blend in all of my recipes. After much experimenting, I chose white rice flour, tapioca flour and potato starch as my base. Next I had to figure out the proportions. The cakes quickly let me know that a higher ratio of tapioca flour to potato starch yielded cakes that had more springiness and were less crumbly. I added salt to my flour blend to round out the flavors. If you're using the flour blend in everyday cooking, there's no need to adjust the salt in your recipes. The last ingredient is xanthan gum, a natural emulsifier and stabilizer.

Since my family eats its share of pancakes and waffles, I also wanted be able to have a pancake mix ready, especially for a sleepy Sunday morning. So once I was satisfied with my all-purpose flour, I set out to create a pancake mix. The result was a mix that is not supersweet, which makes it good for other uses, such as coating foods for frying.

You can find all of the ingredients you'll need for both the flour blend and the pancake mix at your local natural foods store, or you can order them online directly from my two favorite suppliers: Bob's Red Mill (bobsredmill.com) for the white rice flour, potato starch and xanthan gum; and Shiloh Farms (shilohfarms.com) for the tapioca flour. Be sure to buy potato starch, not potato flour—a mistake I made that turned into a morning of laughs when I couldn't seem to ever add enough liquid to a pancake batter I was stirring together.

I like to have good-size containers full of all-purpose flour blend and pancake mix on hand. I store them in airtight containers in a cool, dry place. If you have enough room, you can store them in your refrigerator or freezer. Just shake or whisk before using.

ingredients

OTHER GLUTEN-FREE AND DAIRY-FREE INGREDIENTS I USE THAT YOU PROBABLY ALREADY HAVE ON HAND:

Rice milk, such as Rice Dream

Vegetable shortening, such as Crisco

Vegetable oil

Corn or rice pasta, such as Sam Mills Pasta d'Oro, Bionaturae, Lundberg, Ancient Harvest or DeBoles

Rice cereal, such as Erewhon, processed into crumbs

substitution chart

The recipes in my cookbook are flexible and accessible to everyone. You can cook up a recipe as is or substitute any ingredient to better fit your lifestyle. Since my recipes use mostly conventional ingredients straight from the supermarket, the substitution list is short.

I USE...	YOU COULD ALSO USE...
Silvana's All-Purpose Flour	All-purpose flour
Silvana's Pancake Mix	Store-bought pancake mix
Rice milk	Other nondairy milk, cow's milk
Vegetable shortening	Unsalted butter
Vegetable oil	Melted unsalted butter
Corn or rice pasta	Durum wheat pasta
Rice cereal crumbs	Dried bread crumbs

kitchen tools

in the drawer...

1. **12-inch balloon whisk** (such as Cuisipro)

   The most important task a whisk performs in my kitchen is sifting. Instead of using a flour sifter or a sieve, I use a whisk to aerate the flour, which makes baked goods lighter.

2. **1½-inch ice cream scoop** (such as Matfer Bourgeat or Norpro)

   A scoop isn't just for ice cream. I use it for measuring out cookie dough onto a baking sheet and filling muffin liners with batter.

3. **Large silicone spatula spoon** (such as Le Creuset)

   Wooden spoons have their well-worn place, but a silicone spatula gets every last bit of batter from a bowl and is great for gently stirring scrambled eggs and getting into saucepan corners.

4. **Immersion blender** (such as Cuisinart)

   This is all you need to transform a soup or sauce from chunky to smooth and creamy—and it takes up less space than a regular blender or food processor.

5. **Set of measuring cups and spoons** (such as RSVP measuring cups and KitchenArt adjustable measuring spoons)

   In any baking recipe, accuracy is important. If you're just starting to cook, measuring out ingredients for any recipe teaches you about proportions.

6. **Tapered wooden rolling pin** (such as Vic Firth)

   I've tried them all—with handles, silicone, marble—and none gives me better control than a classic tapered wooden rolling pin.

7. **Digital cooking thermometer and timer** (such as Polder)

   Many distractions fill my kitchen, so I depend on this timer to save my life—and my recipes. I use the thermometer whenever I'm cooking a roast.

the basics

on the stove...

1. **14-inch oven mitt with magnet**
    (such as Le Creuset)

    When I owned my Italian bakery, I wanted long oven
    mitts to protect myself and my bakers from burns, an
    inevitable part of daily baking. Not only were these
    mitts long, they were also magnetic, which meant we
    could throw them against the oven and they'd always
    be there when we needed them.

2. **5½-quart round Dutch oven**
    (such as Le Creuset)

    When I graduated from college, this was all I wanted.
    Later, when I got married, I asked for more. I like the
    flexibility a Dutch oven gives me. I can go from stove
    to oven to fridge with one cooking vessel.

3. **14-inch by 16-inch baking stone**
    (such as Old Stone Oven)

    I've done my due diligence on this baking stone.
    Many pizzas later, it has outperformed an upside-down
    baking sheet, delivering a crispy, golden-brown crust
    every time.

4. **10¼-inch seasoned cast-iron skillet**
    (such as Lodge)

    I didn't inherit my cast-iron skillet from my grandmother,
    but from my husband. It fries up bacon crispy like
    nothing else and gives my cornbread its much-loved
    crusty edges (turn to page 75 for the recipe; bake in a
    skillet for 25 to 30 minutes).

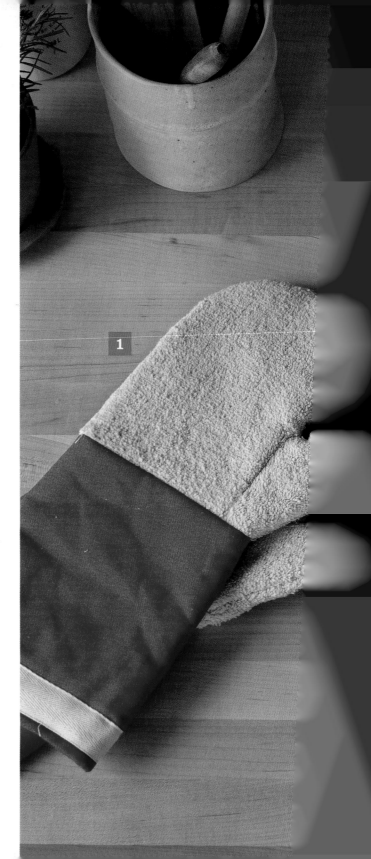

breakfast

BEFORE I'M FULLY AWAKE IN THE MORNING, I'm thinking of breakfast, especially on the weekends. Fluffy pancakes. Warm maple syrup. The smell of bacon that easily stays with us till noon. It's one of my favorite meals of the day—maybe because I'm more sweet than savory. Lucky for me, my family feels the same. After I've had my cup of coffee, I'm ready to negotiate what's on the menu. Isaiah loves his pancakes and French toast, and Chiara her waffles. Breakfast has become my family's well-honed ritual—a big table filled with food, lots of sticky fingers and sometimes, yes, sometimes, even a remote control. Our breakfast time is important, and I don't want that to change. I'm not going to deny Isaiah that singular pleasure he gets not only from food, but from all of us eating together. I want to make new food memories even better than our old ones. Maybe I'm overcompensating, but I don't just make plain pancakes—I make banana pancakes and gingerbread pancakes and s'mores pancakes and griddled corn cakes. And making waffle recipes has opened my eyes to the everlasting possibilities of what I can cook in a waffle iron, including hash brown potatoes. Then there are the muffins and breakfast cakes and eggs every which way, and, of course, Isaiah's own hot chocolate.

"For my family, eating breakfast together can be more realistic than sitting down to dinner."

"I have a small s'mores addiction. I can pretty much turn any sweet recipe into a s'mores version. No apologies."

s'mores pancakes
with marshmallow sauce

The marshmallow sauce is easy to make and perfect drizzled over the pancakes.

MAKES 20 (3-inch/7.5-cm) pancakes   PREP TIME 10 minutes   COOK TIME 15 minutes

pancakes

2 cups Silvana's Pancake Mix (page 15)

¼ teaspoon salt

2 tablespoons packed light brown sugar

2 large eggs, at room temperature

1¼ cups rice milk

1 tablespoon unsulphured molasses

1 tablespoon honey

2 tablespoons vegetable oil, plus more for greasing

½ cup mini chocolate chips

marshmallow sauce

1 cup marshmallow creme, such as Fluff

2 tablespoons boiling water

1. To make the pancakes, in a large bowl, whisk together the pancake mix, salt and brown sugar.

2. In a medium bowl, whisk together the eggs, milk, molasses, honey and oil. Add to the dry ingredients and stir until just combined. Fold in the chocolate chips.

3. Heat a large nonstick skillet over medium heat. Using a paper towel, lightly grease with oil. Pour the batter about ¼ cup at a time into the pan and cook the pancakes until golden and set, about 2 minutes on each side.

4. Meanwhile, to make the sauce, in a medium bowl, stir together the marshmallow creme and boiling water until smooth. Serve with the pancakes.

breakfast

banana pancakes with warm cinnamon goo

The warm cinnamon goo takes the pancakes over the edge of deliciousness.
If you want an easy weekday breakfast, make extra pancakes to freeze for later.

MAKES 20 (3-inch/7.5-cm) pancakes **PREP TIME** 10 minutes **COOK TIME** 18 minutes

cinnamon goo

1 cup packed light brown sugar

½ teaspoon ground cinnamon

1 cup water

pancakes

2 cups Silvana's Pancake Mix (page 15)

1 banana, mashed

2 teaspoons pure vanilla extract

1 large egg, at room temperature, lightly beaten

1½ cups rice milk

1 tablespoon vegetable oil, plus more for greasing

½ teaspoon ground cinnamon

1. To make the goo, in a medium saucepan combine the brown sugar, cinnamon and water, and bring to a boil over high heat, stirring occasionally. Reduce until thickened, about 10 minutes; keep warm.

2. Meanwhile, to make the pancakes, in a medium bowl, stir together the pancake mix, banana, vanilla, egg, milk, oil and cinnamon until just combined.

3. Heat a large nonstick skillet over medium heat. Using a paper towel, lightly grease with oil. Pour the batter about ¼ cup at a time onto the pan and cook each pancake until golden and set, about 2 minutes on each side. To serve, drizzle the warm cinnamon goo over the pancakes.

"On the weekends, I like to wake up with the kids and cook a breakfast feast. Chiara cracks my eggs, and Isaiah is the designated pancake flipper."

blueberry-lemon sourdough pancakes

Yeast gives these pancakes a lovely airiness and slight sourness, which is then heightened by a buttermilk-like mixture of milk and apple cider vinegar. The best thing about this pancake batter is that you can refrigerate it overnight. Then all you have to do in the morning is bring it to room temperature.

MAKES 20 (3-inch/7.5-cm) pancakes PREP TIME 10 minutes (plus standing) COOK TIME 25 minutes

1¾ cups rice milk

2 teaspoons apple cider vinegar

2 cups Silvana's Pancake Mix (page 15)

1 (¼-ounce/7.5-g) package active dry yeast

2 large eggs, at room temperature, lightly beaten

¼ cup vegetable oil, plus more for greasing

2 teaspoons pure vanilla extract

Finely grated zest of 1 lemon

1 cup blueberries, plus more for topping

Maple syrup, warmed, for serving

1. In a small bowl, stir together the milk and vinegar.

2. In a large bowl, whisk together the pancake mix and yeast. Add the eggs, oil, vanilla, lemon zest and milk mixture; whisk until just combined. Cover with plastic wrap and let stand at room temperature for 30 minutes.

3. Heat a large nonstick skillet over medium heat. Using a paper towel, lightly grease with oil. Gently fold the blueberries into the batter. Pour the batter, about ¼ cup at a time, into the pan, top with a few berries and cook pancakes until golden and set, about 2 minutes on each side. Serve with warm maple syrup.

THE THIEF LORD

Isaiah's Pumpkin Muffins with Crumble Topping (page 46)
and Isaiah's Whipped Hot Cocoaccino (page 56)

Isaiah's gingerbread pancakes with apple-cinnamon slaw

The coffee brings out the spicy, gingery flavor in the pancakes. Go ahead and use decaf if you're serving them to kids. Also, you can swap pears for the apples in the slaw.

MAKES 20 (3-inch/7.5-cm) pancakes PREP TIME 15 minutes COOK TIME 15 minutes

pancakes

2 cups Silvana's Pancake Mix (page 15)

½ teaspoon baking soda

2 tablespoons packed light brown sugar

1 tablespoon unsweetened cocoa powder

1½ teaspoons ground ginger

1 teaspoon pumpkin pie spice

2 large eggs, at room temperature, separated

1 cup rice milk

½ cup plus 1 tablespoon brewed coffee, at room temperature

2 tablespoons vegetable oil, plus more for greasing

1 tablespoon unsulphured molasses

slaw

3 apples, cored and coarsely grated

2 tablespoons fresh lemon juice

1 tablespoon honey

¼ cup golden raisins

½ cup pecans, toasted

Maple syrup, warmed, for serving

1. To make the pancakes, in a large bowl, whisk together the pancake mix, baking soda, brown sugar, cocoa powder, ginger and pumpkin pie spice.

2. In a medium bowl, beat the egg whites until soft peaks form.

3. In a separate medium bowl, whisk together the egg yolks, milk, coffee, oil and molasses; add to the pancake mix mixture and stir until just combined. Gently fold in the beaten egg whites.

4. Heat a large nonstick skillet over medium-low heat. Using a paper towel, lightly grease with oil. Pour the batter about ¼ cup at a time into the pan and cook until the pancakes are golden and set, about 2 minutes on each side.

5. Meanwhile, to make the slaw, in a medium bowl, stir together the apples, lemon juice, honey, raisins and pecans. Serve the pancakes with maple syrup and the slaw.

"I was making cornbread when I realized that I could pour the batter into a hot skillet and eat corn cakes instead."

griddled corn cakes with strawberry syrup

You can drizzle the corn cakes with the strawberry syrup, but they're also nice plain and served with dinner. The medium-grind cornmeal gives the pancakes a buttery, rich flavor.

MAKES 20 (3-inch/7.5-cm) pancakes   PREP TIME 5 minutes   COOK TIME 15 minutes

corn cakes

1¼ cups rice milk

2 teaspoons apple cider vinegar

1 cup Silvana's Pancake Mix (page 15)

1 cup cornmeal, preferably medium grind

½ teaspoon salt

2 large eggs, at room temperature, lightly beaten

¼ cup vegetable oil, plus more for greasing

syrup

1 cup strawberry jelly

¼ cup water

1. To make the corn cakes, in a small bowl, stir together the milk and vinegar.

2. In a medium bowl, whisk together the pancake mix, cornmeal and salt. Add the milk mixture, eggs and oil; stir until just combined.

3. Heat a large nonstick skillet over medium heat. Using a paper towel, lightly grease with oil. Pour the batter about ¼ cup at a time into the pan and cook until the pancakes are golden and set, about 2 minutes on each side.

4. Meanwhile, to make the syrup, in a small saucepan, cook the jelly and water over low heat, stirring occasionally, until syrupy. Serve with the corn cakes.

chocolate chip–banana split belgian waffles with wet walnuts and hot fudge sauce

To keep the waffles warm, place them uncovered on a wire rack set on a baking sheet in a 200°F oven until you're ready to serve breakfast.

SERVES 6 PREP TIME 20 minutes COOK TIME 25 minutes

wet walnuts
½ cup light corn syrup

½ cup sugar

½ cup cold water

1 cup chopped walnuts

fudge sauce
1 cup mini chocolate chips

2 tablespoons all-vegetable shortening

½ cup boiling water

2 tablespoons light corn syrup

1 cup sugar

1 tablespoon pure vanilla extract

¼ teaspoon salt

waffles
2 cups Silvana's Pancake Mix (page 15)

½ teaspoon salt

½ teaspoon ground cinnamon

1 large egg, at room temperature

2 tablespoons vegetable oil

1½ cups rice milk

3 bananas—1 mashed and 2 diagonally sliced ¼ inch (0.5 cm) thick

1 tablespoon pure vanilla extract

½ cup mini chocolate chips

1. To make the wet walnuts, in a medium saucepan, stir together the corn syrup, sugar and water. Bring to a boil over medium heat, stirring occasionally. Boil for 2 minutes, without stirring. Stir in the walnuts and return to a boil. Remove from the heat and let cool to room temperature, about 15 minutes.

2. To make the sauce, in another medium saucepan over low heat, combine the chocolate chips, shortening and boiling water; stir until smooth. Stir in the corn syrup and sugar. Increase the heat to medium and bring to a boil, stirring occasionally; let boil for 6 minutes. Stir in the vanilla and salt. Cover and keep warm.

3. Preheat a Belgian waffle iron to medium-high heat. To make the waffles, in a large bowl, whisk together the pancake mix, salt, cinnamon, egg, oil, milk, mashed banana and vanilla. Add the chocolate chips; stir until just combined.

4. Grease the waffle iron with nonstick cooking spray. Pour a heaping ⅓ cup batter into each waffle iron quarter, spreading the batter out to the edges. Close and cook until crisp, about 4 minutes. Repeat with the remaining batter.

5. To serve, top the waffles with the banana slices, wet walnuts and hot fudge sauce.

"On the weekends, we used to make regular stops at the International House of Pancakes. This home-cooked breakfast satisfies those over-the-top cravings."

cinnamon-toasted belgian waffles

These waffles have the characteristics of cinnamon toast—crunchy on top, bready to the bite and just the right balance of sugar and spice. If you grew up on cinnamon toast, you know there's nothing quite like it—until you take your first bite into these waffles. To keep the waffles warm, place them uncovered on a wire rack set on a baking sheet in a 200°F oven.

SERVES 4 PREP TIME 5 minutes COOK TIME 4 minutes

¼ cup granulated sugar

¼ cup packed light brown sugar

1½ teaspoons ground cinnamon

2 cups Silvana's Pancake Mix (page 15)

2 large eggs, at room temperature, lightly beaten

¼ cup vegetable oil

1 tablespoon pure vanilla extract

1½ cups rice milk

Maple syrup, warmed, for serving

1. In a small bowl, mix together the granulated sugar, brown sugar and 1 teaspoon cinnamon.

2. Preheat a Belgian waffle iron to medium-high heat. In a large bowl, whisk together the pancake mix and remaining ½ teaspoon cinnamon.

3. In a small bowl, whisk together the eggs, oil, vanilla and milk; add to the pancake mix and stir until just combined.

4. Grease the waffle iron with nonstick cooking spray. Pour a heaping ⅓ cup batter into each waffle iron quarter, spreading the batter out to the edges. Sprinkle generously with the cinnamon sugar; close and cook until crisp, about 4 minutes. Serve with warm maple syrup.

honey-nut-and-banana crepes

To keep the crepes warm while cooking, stack them on top of each other on a baking sheet and place them in a 200°F oven.

SERVES 4 to 6   PREP TIME 10 minutes (plus standing)   COOK TIME 20 minutes

crepes

⅔ cup Silvana's
All-Purpose Flour (page 15)

1 teaspoon sugar

Finely grated zest of ½ lemon

¼ teaspoon salt

2 large eggs, at room
temperature, lightly beaten

1 teaspoon pure vanilla extract

1 tablespoon vegetable oil,
plus more for greasing

1 cup rice milk

filling

½ cup sugar

1 tablespoon honey

2 tablespoons water

3 bananas, peeled and
diagonally sliced about
¼ inch (0.5 cm) thick

1 cup chopped walnuts

1. To make the crepes, in a medium bowl, whisk together the flour, sugar, lemon zest and salt. Add the eggs, vanilla, oil and milk; whisk until combined. Cover and let stand for 20 minutes or refrigerate overnight.

2. Heat a 10-inch (25-cm) nonstick skillet over medium heat. Using a paper towel, lightly grease with oil. Pour ⅓ cup of the batter into the center of the pan, tilting to spread evenly; cook until golden around the edges, about 1 minute on each side. Remove from the pan and stack on a plate. Repeat with the remaining batter.

3. Meanwhile, to make the filling, in a separate medium nonstick skillet, cook the sugar, honey and water over high heat until bubbling and light amber in color, about 6 minutes. Add the bananas and walnuts and cook over medium-high heat, turning occasionally, until caramelized, about 3 minutes.

4. To serve, place a crepe on a plate, top with one-quarter of the banana-nut mixture and roll up burrito-style. Repeat with the remaining crepes and filling.

*"I love the honey-nut flavor combination.
Here I caramelize nuts and bananas on
the stovetop with honey, then stuff everything
into crepes."*

"*By now my family knows that if they want to eat a doughnut or two, they'd better move fast.*"

chocolate-dipped chocolate doughnuts

This is my oversimplified definition of heaven—chocolate on chocolate.

MAKES 12 doughnuts   PREP TIME 15 minutes   COOK TIME 18 minutes

doughnuts

1½ tablespoons instant
espresso coffee

¾ cup boiling water

2 large eggs, at room
temperature, lightly beaten

6 tablespoons vegetable oil

1 tablespoon pure
vanilla extract

1½ cups Silvana's
All-Purpose Flour (page 15)

½ cup unsweetened
cocoa powder

1½ teaspoons baking powder

¾ teaspoon baking soda

¾ teaspoon salt

¾ cup packed light
brown sugar

¾ cup granulated sugar

glaze

¼ cup boiling water

6 ounces semisweet chocolate,
chopped (about 1 cup)

2¼ cups confectioners' sugar

1½ tablespoons light
corn syrup

1 teaspoon pure vanilla extract

Rainbow sprinkles,
for topping

1. Preheat the oven to 350°F. Grease two nonstick 6-doughnut baking pans with nonstick cooking spray. To make the doughnuts, in a medium bowl, whisk together the coffee and boiling water; let cool completely. Whisk in the eggs, oil and vanilla.

2. In a large bowl, whisk together the flour, cocoa powder, baking powder, baking soda, salt, brown sugar and granulated sugar. Whisk the egg mixture into the flour mixture until just combined; fill each doughnut cup about three-quarters full. Bake until springy to the touch and a toothpick inserted in the center comes out clean, about 18 minutes. Let cool completely in the pans set on a wire rack.

3. To make the glaze, in a medium bowl, stir together the boiling water and chocolate until melted. Sift in the confectioners' sugar, and add the corn syrup and vanilla; stir until smooth.

4. Set a rack over a baking sheet. Dip the doughnuts in the glaze and set on the prepared rack; top with sprinkles.

"These remind me of the doughnuts we get at a farm near our house in upstate New York—cakey, but with a moist crumb."

sugar-and-spiced doughnuts

There's just nothing like a warm doughnut, except maybe a warm doughnut right after it's been coated with spiced sugar. You'll have spiced sugar left over, which is great stirred into tea or sprinkled over ice cream (like the pumpkin ice cream on page 209).

MAKES 10 doughnuts   PREP TIME 10 minutes   COOK TIME 15 minutes

doughnuts

1½ cups Silvana's
All-Purpose Flour (page 15)

1 cup sugar

2 teaspoons baking powder

½ teaspoon salt

¼ teaspoon ground cinnamon

¼ teaspoon ground nutmeg

2 large eggs, at room
temperature

¼ cup vegetable oil

½ cup rice milk

spiced sugar

½ cup sugar

2 teaspoons ground cinnamon

½ teaspoon ground nutmeg

¼ teaspoon salt

⅛ teaspoon ground cloves

1. Preheat the oven to 350°F. Grease two nonstick 6-doughnut baking pans with nonstick cooking spray. To make the doughnuts, in a large bowl, whisk together the flour, sugar, baking powder, salt, cinnamon and nutmeg.

2. In a medium bowl, whisk together the eggs, oil and milk until smooth. Add to the flour mixture and whisk until combined; fill each doughnut cup about three-quarters full. Bake until golden and a toothpick inserted in the center comes out clean, about 15 minutes. Let cool slightly in the pans.

3. Meanwhile, to make the spiced sugar, in a small bowl, stir together the sugar, cinnamon, nutmeg, salt and cloves. Dredge the warm doughnuts in the spiced sugar to coat.

banana doughnuts
with banana frosting

If you don't have a doughnut pan, you can bake this batter in muffin tins in a
350°F oven until a toothpick inserted in the center comes out dry, about 20 minutes.

MAKES 12 doughnuts **PREP TIME** 20 minutes **COOK TIME** 12 to 15 minutes

doughnuts

**1¼ cups Silvana's
All-Purpose Flour (page 15)**

2 teaspoons baking powder

½ teaspoon salt

**1½ teaspoons ground
cinnamon**

**2 large eggs, at room
temperature**

1 cup granulated sugar

**1½ cups mashed ripe
bananas (about 3 bananas)**

**2 teaspoons pure
vanilla extract**

½ cup vegetable oil

frosting

**¼ cup all-vegetable shortening,
at room temperature**

2½ cups confectioners' sugar

**½ cup mashed banana
(about ½ banana)**

¼ teaspoon ground cinnamon

**2 teaspoons pure
vanilla extract**

½ teaspoon fresh lemon juice

1. Preheat the oven to 350°F. Grease two nonstick 6-doughnut baking pans with nonstick cooking spray. To make the doughnuts, in a large bowl, whisk together the flour, baking powder, salt and cinnamon.

2. In a small bowl, whisk together the eggs, granulated sugar, bananas, vanilla and oil. Stir the wet ingredients into the dry until just combined; fill each doughnut cup about three-quarters full. Bake until golden and a toothpick inserted in the center comes out clean, 12 to 15 minutes. Let cool completely in the pans set on a wire rack.

3. Meanwhile, to make the frosting, in a small bowl, beat together the shortening and confectioners' sugar until fluffy. Beat in the banana, cinnamon, vanilla and lemon juice. Spread the frosting over the cooled doughnuts.

hash brown belgian waffles with apple sausage and fried eggs

This recipe has diner food written all over it. The dried apples in the sausage patties add just the right amount of sweet, caramelized flavor.

SERVES 4 PREP TIME 20 minutes COOK TIME 30 minutes

1 pound (500 g) sweet Italian sausage, casings removed

⅓ cup dried apples, finely chopped

1 tablespoon packed light brown sugar

¾ teaspoon dry mustard

¼ teaspoon paprika

Salt and pepper

3 tablespoons vegetable oil

3 Yukon Gold potatoes (about 1½ pounds/750 g)—peeled, grated and wrung dry

½ medium onion, grated

4 large eggs, at room temperature

Ketchup, for serving

1. In a medium bowl, mix together the sausage, apples, brown sugar, mustard, paprika, ½ teaspoon salt and ⅛ teaspoon pepper; shape into four 4-inch (0.8-cm) patties, about ⅓ inch (10 cm) thick.

2. In a large nonstick skillet, heat 1 tablespoon oil over medium heat. Add the patties and cook until browned and cooked through, about 4 minutes on each side. Cover loosely with aluminum foil to keep warm.

3. In a small bowl, mix together the potatoes, onion, 1 tablespoon oil and ¾ teaspoon salt.

4. Preheat a Belgian waffle iron to medium-high heat. Grease the waffle iron with nonstick cooking spray. Mound ½ cup of the potato mixture in each waffle quarter; close and cook until golden and crisp, about 10 minutes.

5. Meanwhile, in a large skillet, heat the remaining 1 tablespoon oil over medium heat. Crack the eggs into the skillet and season with salt and pepper; cook, turning once, until the whites are set and yolks are slightly runny, about 3 minutes.

6. To serve, place a waffle on each of four plates; top with a sausage patty and a fried egg. Serve with ketchup.

"I serve up my sausage and eggs with crispy hash brown waffles, which taste better than a side of fries."

"Isaiah and I have hit our share of drive-thrus for onion rings alone. There's no need now with this speedy, satisfying recipe."

onion ring–stuffed souffléed omelet

While you make the omelets, keep the onion rings warm in a 200°F oven.

SERVES 4 **PREP TIME** 10 minutes **COOK TIME** 12 minutes

4 cups vegetable oil, for frying

2 cups Silvana's Pancake Mix (page 15)

1 teaspoon chili powder

Salt

3½ cups cold seltzer

2 large onions, cut crosswise into ½-inch (1-cm) slices and separated into rings

4 tablespoons extra-virgin olive oil

8 large eggs, at room temperature

Ketchup, for serving

1. Preheat the oven to 200°F. In a large pot or deep fryer, heat the vegetable oil to 380°F.

2. In a large bowl, whisk together the pancake mix, chili powder and 1 teaspoon salt. Add the seltzer and whisk until smooth.

3. Working in batches, coat the onion rings with the batter, letting any excess drip into the bowl; carefully add to the hot oil and fry, turning once, until golden and crisp, about 2 minutes. Drain on paper towels and sprinkle with salt. Repeat with the remaining onion rings and batter.

4. Add 1 tablespoon olive oil to an 8-inch (20-cm) nonstick skillet over medium-high heat and swirl to coat; heat until hot but not smoking. Meanwhile, using an immersion blender and working with 2 eggs at a time, beat for 1 minute; pour into the skillet, season with about ¼ teaspoon salt and cook until the edges are set, about 1 minute. Flip and cook for 30 seconds more. Transfer to a plate, top with some of the onion rings and fold in half. Loosely cover with aluminum foil to keep warm. Repeat with the remaining olive oil, eggs and onion rings. Serve with ketchup.

scrambled eggs and ham–stuffed corn-chive crepe wraps

These wraps make great on-the-go breakfasts. Give the crepe batter a stir before pouring it into the skillet to mix the heavier ingredients that settle at the bottom of the bowl. To keep the crepes warm, stack them on top of each other on a baking sheet and place them in a 200°F oven.

SERVES 4 to 6 **PREP TIME** 10 minutes **COOK TIME** 15 minutes (plus standing)

⅓ cup Silvana's
All-Purpose Flour (page 15)

⅓ cup cornmeal,
preferably medium grind

2 tablespoons finely
chopped fresh chives

¾ teaspoon salt

2 tablespoons vegetable oil,
plus more for greasing

1 cup plus 2 tablespoons
rice milk

6 large eggs, at room
temperature

4 ounces (125 g) deli-sliced
ham, thinly sliced into strips

1. In a medium bowl, whisk together the flour, cornmeal, chives and ¼ teaspoon salt. Add 1 tablespoon oil, 1 cup milk and 2 eggs; whisk until combined. Cover and let stand for 20 minutes or refrigerate overnight.

2. Heat a 10-inch (25-cm) nonstick skillet over medium heat. Using a paper towel, lightly grease with oil. Pour ⅓ cup batter into the center of the pan, tilting to spread evenly; cook until golden around the edges, about 1 minute on each side. Remove the crepe from the pan and stack on a plate. Repeat with the remaining batter.

3. Meanwhile, in a separate medium skillet, heat the remaining 1 tablespoon oil over medium heat. Add the ham and cook, stirring, until golden, about 2 minutes. In a small bowl, whisk together the remaining 4 eggs, remaining 2 tablespoons milk and remaining ½ teaspoon salt; add to the skillet and cook, stirring occasionally, until set, about 3 minutes.

4. To serve, place a crepe on a clean work surface and across the center, top with one-quarter of the scrambled eggs and one-quarter of the ham; roll up burrito-style. Repeat with the remaining crepes, eggs and ham.

breakfast

"My kids and I love this hearty but light egg pie for breakfast or lunch, hot from the oven or at room temperature."

potato-crusted bacon bits and egg pie

The best way to keep enough bacon on hand is to freeze it in individual strips sandwiched between sheets of plastic wrap, folded and tucked into a resealable freezer bag. This also makes it a lot easier to chop. For a change, add 2 teaspoons chopped fresh rosemary to the potatoes before frying.

SERVES 4 to 6　**PREP TIME** 15 minutes (plus standing)　**COOK TIME** 36 minutes

6 slices bacon, cut into ½-inch (1-cm) pieces

2 Yukon Gold potatoes (about 12 ounces/375 g)— peeled, grated and wrung dry

1 teaspoon paprika

Salt and pepper

3 large eggs, at room temperature, separated

½ cup rice milk

1 teaspoon yellow mustard

1. Preheat the oven to 350°F. In a 10-inch (25-cm) ovenproof nonstick skillet, cook the bacon over medium heat until crispy and the fat has rendered, about 3 minutes. Using a slotted spoon, remove the bacon from the pan; drain on paper towels.

2. In medium bowl, toss together the potatoes with the paprika and ½ teaspoon salt. Add to the skillet with the rendered bacon fat, spreading the potatoes evenly on the bottom. Cook, without stirring, until crisp on the bottom, about 8 minutes.

3. Meanwhile, in another medium bowl, whisk the egg whites until soft peaks form. In a large bowl, whisk together the egg yolks, milk, mustard and reserved bacon; season with ¼ teaspoon each salt and pepper. Fold in the egg whites; pour over the potatoes and bake until puffed and golden, about 25 minutes. Let stand for about 5 minutes before slicing.

breakfast

Isaiah's pumpkin muffins with crumble topping

If you make these muffins around the holidays, stir a handful of dried cranberries or ¼ cup chopped walnuts into the batter. You can also make pumpkin muffin tops with this recipe—just use a muffin-top pan and bake for about 10 minutes.

MAKES 12 muffins   PREP TIME 20 minutes   COOK TIME 25 minutes

topping

¼ cup Silvana's
All-Purpose Flour (page 15)

¼ cup packed light
brown sugar

¼ cup granulated sugar

½ teaspoon pumpkin pie spice

4 tablespoons all-vegetable
shortening

muffins

1¾ cups Silvana's
All-Purpose Flour (page 15)

2 teaspoons baking powder

2 teaspoons pumpkin pie spice

¾ teaspoon salt

2 large eggs, at room
temperature

1 cup canned pure
pumpkin puree

1 cup granulated sugar

½ cup vegetable oil

1 tablespoon pure
vanilla extract

Confectioners' sugar,
for sprinkling

1. Preheat the oven to 350°F. Line a 12-cup muffin pan with paper liners. To make the topping, in a medium bowl, whisk together the flour, brown sugar, granulated sugar and pumpkin pie spice. Add the shortening and, using your fingers or a fork, blend together until coarse crumbs form.

2. To make the muffins, in a large bowl, whisk together the flour, baking powder, pumpkin pie spice and salt.

3. In a medium bowl, whisk together the eggs, pumpkin puree, granulated sugar, oil and vanilla until smooth. Add to the flour mixture; stir until just combined. Pour the batter into the prepared muffin pan until each cup is two-thirds full; top each with crumble topping. Bake until the muffins are springy to the touch and a toothpick inserted in the center comes out clean, 20 to 25 minutes. Let cool in the pan set on a wire rack. Using a sieve, sprinkle with confectioners' sugar.

carrot-pineapple muffins

If you don't have time to bake on weekday mornings, freeze muffin batter so you can bake whenever you want. Just fill muffin liners with batter and freeze until firm, then transfer to a resealable freezer bag. When you bake the muffins, add about 10 minutes to the baking time.

MAKES 12 muffins   PREP TIME 15 minutes   COOK TIME 25 minutes

1 cup Silvana's
All-Purpose Flour (page 15)

1 teaspoon baking powder

½ teaspoon baking soda

¼ teaspoon salt

½ teaspoon ground cinnamon

2 large eggs, at room
temperature

1 cup packed light
brown sugar

⅓ cup vegetable oil

2 teaspoons pure
vanilla extract

1 cup loosely packed shredded
carrot (about 1 large carrot)

½ cup chopped fresh or
canned pineapple, drained

½ cup walnuts,
coarsely chopped

1. Preheat the oven to 350°F. Line a 12-cup muffin pan with paper liners. In a medium bowl, whisk together the flour, baking powder, baking soda, salt and cinnamon.

2. In a large bowl, whisk together the eggs, brown sugar, oil and vanilla until smooth. Stir in the carrot, pineapple and walnuts. Stir in the flour mixture until just combined. Pour the batter into the prepared muffin pan until each cup is two-thirds full. Bake until the muffins are springy to the touch and a toothpick inserted in the center comes out clean, about 25 minutes. Let cool in the pan set on a wire rack.

"The kids love anything with some semblance of frosting. I love that they're eating fruit in the morning."

fruit salad muffins with lemon drizzle

These are superlight, yet full of flavor, with a refreshing lemon drizzle finish. As with any fruit salad, use whatever you have on hand.

MAKES 12 muffins PREP TIME 25 minutes (plus cooling) COOK TIME 30 minutes

1½ cups Silvana's
All-Purpose Flour (page 15)

2 teaspoons baking powder

½ teaspoon salt

2 large eggs, at room
temperature, separated

1 cup granulated sugar

½ cup vegetable oil

1 teaspoon pure vanilla extract

2 tablespoons rice milk

Finely grated zest of 1 lemon

½ cup water

1½ cups mixed fruit
(such as apples, strawberries,
bananas and mango), cut into
½-inch (1-cm) pieces

¾ cup confectioners'
sugar, sifted

1½ tablespoons fresh
lemon juice

1. Preheat the oven to 350°F. Line a 12-cup muffin pan with paper liners. In a large bowl, whisk together the flour, baking powder and salt.

2. In a small bowl, beat the egg whites until small peaks form.

3. In a medium bowl, whisk together the egg yolks, granulated sugar, oil, vanilla, milk, lemon zest and water until smooth. Add to the flour mixture and whisk until just combined. Fold in the fruit, then fold in the egg whites. Pour the batter into the prepared muffin pan until each cup is two-thirds full. Bake until the muffins are springy to the touch and a toothpick inserted in the center comes out clean, 28 to 30 minutes. Let cool completely in the pan set on a wire rack.

4. Meanwhile, in a small bowl, stir together the confectioners' sugar and lemon juice until smooth. Drizzle over the cooled muffins.

breakfast

berry corn muffins

The berries in these muffins add a bit of tartness. You can also stir some lemon or orange zest into the batter before baking for a nice citrusy flavor.

MAKES 12 muffins PREP TIME 10 minutes COOK TIME 25 minutes

¾ cup cornmeal, preferably medium grind

1 cup Silvana's All-Purpose Flour (page 15)

2 teaspoons baking powder

¾ teaspoon salt

1 cup mixed berries

2 large eggs, at room temperature

½ cup sugar, plus more for sprinkling

½ cup rice milk

½ cup vegetable oil

1. Preheat the oven to 375°F. Line a 12-cup muffin pan with paper liners. In a medium bowl, whisk together the cornmeal, flour, baking powder and salt. Add the berries; gently stir to coat.

2. In a small bowl, whisk together the eggs, sugar, milk and oil. Stir into the dry ingredients until just combined. Pour the batter into the prepared muffin pan until each cup is two-thirds full; sprinkle generously with sugar. Bake until the muffins are springy to the touch and a toothpick inserted in the center comes out clean, about 25 minutes. Let cool in the pan set on a wire rack.

"This pancake pie is a slice of summer at your breakfast table. It's cakey on the outside and pudding-like on the inside."

puffy peach pancake pie with caramel maple syrup

In the fall and winter months, substitute apples or even cranberries for the peaches. To keep the edges crispy, grease and sugar the pie plate.

SERVES 6 **PREP TIME** 15 minutes **COOK TIME** 30 minutes

1¼ cups granulated sugar, plus more for coating and sprinkling

2 tablespoons water

3 peaches (about 1¼ pounds/ 625 g)—peeled, pitted and sliced

¼ cup pure maple syrup

2 large eggs, at room temperature

1 cup Silvana's Pancake Mix (page 15)

½ teaspoon salt

¾ cup rice milk

1 teaspoon pure vanilla extract

Confectioners' sugar, for sprinkling

1. Preheat the oven to 400°F. Grease and sugar a 9-inch (23-cm) pie plate. In a large skillet, cook ½ cup granulated sugar with the water over high heat until bubbling and a light amber caramel forms, 4 to 6 minutes. Add the peaches, decrease the heat to medium-high and cook, stirring occasionally, until slightly softened, about 2 minutes. Using a slotted spoon, transfer the peaches to a plate. Stir the maple syrup into the caramel; cover and keep warm.

2. Meanwhile, combine the eggs, remaining ¾ cup granulated sugar, pancake mix, salt, milk and vanilla in a blender; blend until smooth. Pour half the batter into the prepared pie plate, top evenly with the peaches and cover with the remaining batter; sprinkle generously with granulated sugar. Bake until the pancake pie is set and golden, about 30 minutes. Using a sieve, sprinkle with confectioners' sugar and serve with the caramel maple syrup.

cherry turnovers with cinnamon glaze

If you're using shortening from a can, measure it first, and then place it in the refrigerator to chill. What every baker working with pastry dough should know is that water is your best friend. If the dough cracks while you're forming the turnover, no worries. Just dab with water and rub back together. Also, when you're filling each turnover, keep the remaining pieces of dough cold in the refrigerator.

MAKES 4 turnovers **PREP TIME** 20 minutes **COOK TIME** 22 minutes

8 ounces (250 g) fresh Bing cherries, pitted and chopped, or 1½ cups frozen cherries, defrosted and drained

2 teaspoons fresh lemon juice

¼ cup granulated sugar, plus more for sprinkling

1½ teaspoons cornstarch

½ teaspoon ground cinnamon

Silvana's All-Purpose Flour (page 15), for sprinkling

About 2 pounds (1 kg) All-Purpose Pie Crust dough (page 213) or store-bought pie crust dough, refrigerated

1 large egg beaten with 1 teaspoon water

¼ cup confectioners' sugar, sifted

1¾ teaspoons water

1. Preheat the oven to 400°F. Line a baking sheet with parchment paper. In a medium bowl, mix together the cherries, lemon juice, granulated sugar, cornstarch and ¼ teaspoon cinnamon.

2. Sprinkle a sheet of parchment paper with flour and roll out the dough to form a 14-inch (35-cm) square, about ¼ inch (0.5 cm) thick. Cut into four equal squares. Place about ⅓ cup of the cherry mixture in the center of each square. Brush the edges with some of the egg mixture and fold to enclose, forming a triangle; press the edges to seal. Place about 1 inch (2.5 cm) apart on the prepared baking sheet, brush with the egg mixture and sprinkle generously with granulated sugar. Bake until golden, about 22 minutes. Transfer to a wire rack to cool.

3. Meanwhile, in a small bowl, stir together the confectioners' sugar, water and remaining ¼ teaspoon cinnamon until smooth. Drizzle the cinnamon glaze over the cooled turnovers.

Penny's apple–brown sugar coffee cake

Not all apple cakes taste the same. This one is a really good cake—a perfect mix of sweet apple and spiced chocolate crumb.

SERVES 8 **PREP TIME** 10 minutes **COOK TIME** 45 minutes

1 cup plus 2 teaspoons Silvana's All-Purpose Flour (page 15)

2 teaspoons baking powder

¼ teaspoon salt

¾ cup packed light brown sugar

¼ cup mini chocolate chips

½ cup chopped walnuts

1 teaspoon ground cinnamon

2 large eggs, at room temperature

½ cup granulated sugar

½ cup vegetable oil

2 teaspoons pure vanilla extract

2 large apples—peeled, cored and cut into ½-inch (1-cm) pieces

1. Preheat the oven to 375°F. Lightly grease a 9-inch (23-cm) springform pan or round cake pan. In a large bowl, whisk together 1 cup flour, the baking powder and salt.

2. In a small bowl, toss together the remaining 2 teaspoons flour, ½ cup brown sugar, chocolate chips, walnuts and cinnamon.

3. In another small bowl, whisk together the eggs, granulated sugar and remaining ¼ cup brown sugar until smooth. Whisk in the oil and vanilla. Stir into the flour mixture until just combined. Pour half the batter into the prepared pan, and top with half the apples and half the chocolate chip mixture; repeat with the remaining batter, apples and chocolate chip mixture. Bake the cake until a toothpick inserted in the center comes out clean, about 45 minutes. Let cool in the pan set on a wire rack.

"One morning I was playing around with my mom's classic apple cake recipe. You'll want to trust me on this one."

Isaiah's whipped hot cocoaccino

You can make a double batch of the hot cocoa mix and store it in an airtight container at room temperature for up to 6 months.

SERVES 4 PREP TIME 5 minutes COOK TIME 9 minutes

½ cup confectioners' sugar

¼ cup unsweetened cocoa powder

1½ cups mini chocolate chips

4 cups rice milk

1. In a medium bowl, sift together the confectioners' sugar and cocoa powder; stir in the chocolate chips.

2. Heat the milk in a large saucepan over medium heat and bring to a simmer, about 8 minutes. Whisk in the hot chocolate mix; cook until the chocolate is melted. Remove from the heat and, using an immersion blender on low speed, whip until frothy.

"One Saturday afternoon, Isaiah watched me froth my cappuccino and asked if he could make what he called a 'hot cocoaccino' — creamy, whipped hot chocolate."

Isaiah's fruit smoothie

A banana makes this smoothie creamy rather than icy. You can use water or milk instead of the pear nectar.

SERVES 4 PREP TIME 5 minutes

1½ cups frozen strawberries

1 cup frozen peaches

1 banana, peeled

2 tablespoons honey

1 cup pear nectar

In a blender, combine the strawberries, peaches, banana, honey and pear nectar; blend on high speed until smooth.

breakfast

starters & salads

THE ONE POSITIVE that has come out of Isaiah's food intolerances is his openness to go outside of his food comfort zone and taste new things. He was the classic toddler, with an interest in mostly white foods and few vegetables. It's an addicting food trap, not just for the kid, but for parents who, like me, just need to get dinner done. Isaiah still knows what he likes. Now that means so much more—his eating options are endless, almost. He's still not a big salad eater, but he does like tangy flavors and a good kick of heat. As part of a family that eats out a bunch, my kids have grown familiar with ordering a starter or salad before the main dish. Needless to say, Isaiah and Chiara prefer starters over salads, but there is the occasional surprise, such as when Isaiah takes a fork to lemony-peppery arugula or Chiara jabs a juicy cherry tomato. It always makes me wonder if they'll eat a salad I make at home. What I've learned is that if I top greens with fried shrimp or sliced Buffalo-style chicken or layer them between slices of toasted cornbread, it's definitely an easier sell. Bacon-walnut praline helps, too.

"The first salad I could get Isaiah to eat was a Caesar. These days he's expanded his acceptance of other salad greens and dressings, which is good for the whole family."

"I cook these wings low and slow for perfectly crispy skin and moist, tender chicken every time."

grilled peach BBQ chicken wings

In the winter, swap 1 cup fresh pineapple chunks for the peaches, then bake the wings in a 400°F oven for about 35 minutes.

SERVES 4 **PREP TIME** 20 minutes (plus marinating) **COOK TIME** 35 minutes

2 cups Pineapple–Brown Sugar Barbecue Sauce (page 152) or store-bought barbecue sauce

2 cloves garlic, finely chopped

2 peaches—peeled, pitted and chopped

Salt and pepper

24 chicken wings, separated at the joint and tips discarded

½ cup peach jam, such as Smucker's

2 tablespoons apple cider vinegar

1 tablespoon hot sauce, such as Frank's RedHot, or to taste

Scallions, green parts only, thinly sliced, for topping

1. In a food processor, combine the barbecue sauce and half of the garlic. Add the peaches and process until finely chopped; season with about 1½ teaspoons salt and ¼ teaspoon pepper. Reserve ½ cup for basting. In a resealable plastic bag, toss together the chicken wings and remaining peach barbecue sauce; refrigerate for about 30 minutes.

2. Meanwhile, combine the peach jam, vinegar, remaining garlic, hot sauce and ½ teaspoon salt in a small saucepan. Cook over medium heat until slightly thickened, about 5 minutes; let cool.

3. Preheat a grill or grill pan to low heat. Grill the chicken wings with the grill cover down, turning and basting occasionally with the reserved barbecue sauce until cooked through, about 30 minutes. Top with the scallions and serve with the peach jam dipping sauce.

grilled sausage–stuffed portobellos

You can double the recipe and serve the stuffed mushrooms for dinner. If you're making this recipe in the colder months, bake the mushrooms in a 400°F oven for about 15 minutes.

SERVES 4 **PREP TIME** 10 minutes **COOK TIME** 20 minutes

12 ounces (375 g) Italian sausage, casings removed

1 clove garlic, finely chopped

1 stalk celery, finely chopped

¼ cup pine nuts, lightly toasted

1 teaspoon chopped fresh rosemary

1 large egg, lightly beaten

6 tablespoons rice cereal crumbs

Salt

4 large portobello mushrooms, stems removed

Extra-virgin olive oil, for drizzling

1. Preheat a grill or grill pan to medium-high heat. In a large cast-iron skillet, cook the sausage, breaking up the meat, until almost cooked through, about 3 minutes; drain and transfer to a large bowl. Add the garlic and celery to the skillet and cook, stirring occasionally, until softened, about 2 minutes. Stir into the sausage along with the pine nuts, rosemary, egg, 2 tablespoons cereal crumbs and ¼ teaspoon salt until combined.

2. Generously drizzle the mushrooms with olive oil and grill, gills side down, until the mushrooms release their liquid, 6 to 8 minutes. Remove from the grill, turn gills side up and divide the sausage mixture evenly among the mushrooms; top with the remaining 4 tablespoons cereal crumbs and drizzle generously with olive oil. Return to the grill, cover and cook until golden and cooked through, about 5 minutes.

baked tortilla chips with nectarine, corn and tomato salsa

If you like spicy salsa, keep in some of the jalapeño seeds. The salsa tastes even better the next day.

SERVES 4 **PREP TIME** 20 minutes **COOK TIME** 14 minutes

Twelve 6-inch (15-cm) corn tortillas

Extra-virgin olive oil, for brushing

½ teaspoon paprika

Salt

3 medium tomatoes (about 1 pound/500 g), 2 chopped and 1 quartered

2 nectarines—peeled, pitted and cut into ½-inch (1-cm) pieces

½ cup fresh corn kernels (about ½ ear corn) or frozen corn kernels, thawed

¼ cup finely chopped onion (about 1 small onion)

Finely grated zest and juice of 1 lime

1 clove garlic, peeled

2 jalapeños—stemmed, seeded and finely chopped

¼ cup chopped fresh cilantro or parsley

1. Preheat the oven to 375°F. Line two baking sheets with parchment paper. Brush the tortillas all over with about 2 tablespoons olive oil, then stack and cut into quarters. Place in a single layer on the prepared baking sheets; season with the paprika and about ½ teaspoon salt. Bake until crisp, 12 to 14 minutes.

2. In a medium bowl, stir together the chopped tomatoes, nectarines, corn, onion, lime zest and lime juice.

3. In a food processor, finely chop the quartered tomato, garlic, jalapeños and cilantro. Stir into the tomato-nectarine mixture; season with about 1 teaspoon salt. Serve with the tortilla chips.

sloppy joe–stuffed potato skins

Reserve the scooped-out potato to thicken soup or to make mashed-potato croquettes.

MAKES 12 PREP TIME 5 minutes COOK TIME 1½ hours

6 russet potatoes

2 tablespoons extra-virgin olive oil, plus more for rubbing

Salt and pepper

1 bell pepper, coarsely chopped

½ onion, coarsely chopped

1 pound (500 g) ground beef

¾ cup tomato sauce

1 tablespoon Worcestershire sauce

2 scallions, green parts only, finely chopped, for topping

1. Preheat the oven to 400°F. Using a fork, poke the potatoes in a few places, then rub with olive oil and sprinkle with salt; bake until crispy outside and creamy inside, about 1 hour. Let cool slightly.

2. Halve the potatoes lengthwise and scoop out some of the potato flesh, leaving a skin about ¼ inch (0.5 cm) thick. Rub with olive oil and bake until crispy and golden, about 20 minutes.

3. Meanwhile, in a large, heavy skillet, heat the olive oil over medium heat. Add the bell pepper and onion, and cook, stirring occasionally, until softened, about 5 minutes. Add the beef and cook over medium-high heat, breaking up the meat, until cooked through, about 4 minutes. Stir in the tomato sauce and Worcestershire sauce; season with about 1 teaspoon salt and ¼ teaspoon pepper. Reduce the heat to low and let simmer. To serve, top each potato skin with about 2 heaping tablespoons of sloppy joe and top with the scallions.

sesame shrimp with creamy grilled scallion dip

If you're cooking the shrimp inside, broil them on a wire rack set on a baking sheet. I make a version of this miso marinade at least once a week. Sometimes I leave out the honey or add peanut or almond butter. I use it on everything. I even thin it out with water, chop up some cilantro or parsley and use it as salad dressing.

SERVES 4 PREP TIME 20 minutes (plus marinating) COOK TIME 10 minutes

2 tablespoons chickpea miso, such as Miso Master

5 tablespoons fresh lime juice (about 3 limes)

1 clove garlic, smashed and peeled

2 tablespoons honey

2 teaspoons sriracha hot sauce, or to taste

1 tablespoon plus 1 teaspoon toasted sesame oil

6 tablespoons extra-virgin olive oil

24 jumbo shrimp (about 1¼ pounds/625 g), peeled and deveined, with tails intact

4 small scallions, trimmed

⅓ cup mayonnaise, plus more for brushing

Salt

1 tablespoon sesame seeds, toasted, for topping

1. In a blender, combine the miso, 4 tablespoons lime juice, garlic, honey, hot sauce, 1 tablespoon sesame oil and 4 tablespoons olive oil; blend on high speed until smooth. Transfer to a large resealable plastic bag, add the shrimp and seal; refrigerate for about 30 minutes. Rinse the blender.

2. Preheat a grill to medium-high heat. Brush the scallions with mayonnaise and season with a pinch of salt. Grill, uncovered, turning once, until softened and charred, about 5 minutes.

3. To make the dip, combine the grilled scallions, mayonnaise, remaining 1 tablespoon lime juice, remaining 1 teaspoon sesame oil and remaining 2 tablespoons olive oil in a blender; blend on high speed until smooth. Season with about ¼ teaspoon salt.

4. Thread six shrimp crosswise on each of four skewers. Place on the grill, cover and cook, turning once, until the shrimp are firm and charred, about 5 minutes total. Transfer to a plate and top with the toasted sesame seeds. Serve with the scallion dip.

"I'm not much into frying, but when I do, it's for good reason. These fritters are easy to make and even easier to eat."

corn-shrimp fritters with creamy salsa dip

There are a lot of flavors and textures going on here: sweet corn and shrimp are mixed with heat from the chili powder and cumin, fried until crunchy and ultimately dipped in a creamy, cool salsa. If you don't have a candy thermometer, you can see if the oil is hot enough by dropping a bit of batter into it. If the oil boils, it's ready. While you're frying, keep the cooked fritters warm in a 200°F oven.

MAKES 15 fritters   **PREP TIME** 15 minutes (plus chilling)   **COOK TIME** 12 minutes

1 cup fresh corn kernels (about 1 ear corn) or frozen corn kernels, thawed

1 cup chopped shrimp

2 tablespoons fresh lemon juice

1 teaspoon chili powder

¼ teaspoon ground cumin

2 large eggs, lightly beaten

½ cup Silvana's All-Purpose Flour (page 15)

½ teaspoon salt

2 tablespoons chopped fresh cilantro or parsley

½ cup salsa

¼ cup mayonnaise

Vegetable oil, for frying

1. In a food processor, combine the corn, shrimp, lemon juice, chili powder, cumin, eggs, flour, salt and cilantro; pulse until mostly combined, but still chunky. Transfer to a bowl, cover and refrigerate for about 30 minutes.

2. Meanwhile, in a small bowl, stir together the salsa and mayonnaise; refrigerate.

3. Fill a large pot with about 1 inch (2.5 cm) of oil and heat over medium-high heat until it registers 375°F on a deep-fat thermometer. Working in batches of about four and using a tablespoon, drop the fritter batter into the oil. Fry, turning occasionally, until golden and cooked through, about 3 minutes total. Remove with a slotted spoon and drain on paper towels. Serve with the dip.

buffalo chicken salad

A quick make-ahead tip: You can wash and tear the lettuce 1 day ahead and refrigerate it in a paper towel–lined resealable plastic bag.

SERVES 4 PREP TIME 20 minutes COOK TIME 20 minutes

2 cups rice cereal crumbs

Salt and pepper

4 large eggs

8 chicken tenders
(about 1 pound/500 g)

¼ cup extra-virgin olive oil

¼ cup mayonnaise

2 tablespoons ketchup

1½ teaspoons apple
cider vinegar

2 tablespoons hot sauce, such
as Frank's RedHot, or to taste

2 heads Boston lettuce,
torn into bite-size pieces

4 stalks celery, chopped

1. Preheat the oven to 425°F. In a medium bowl, combine the cereal crumbs, 1½ teaspoons salt and ½ teaspoon pepper. In a shallow bowl, beat the eggs. Coat a chicken tender with the crumbs, dip in the eggs, then coat again with the crumbs; place on a large plate. Repeat with the remaining chicken tenders.

2. In a large skillet, heat the olive oil over medium-high heat until shimmering. Add the chicken tenders and cook in batches, turning once, until golden, about 4 minutes total. Transfer to a baking sheet. Repeat with the remaining chicken, then bake until cooked through, about 8 minutes. Let cool slightly and slice on a diagonal into ½-inch (1-cm) strips.

3. Meanwhile, in a small bowl, combine the mayonnaise, ketchup, vinegar and hot sauce; season with salt and pepper.

4. In a large bowl, toss together the lettuce, celery and about three-quarters of the dressing; top with the chicken and drizzle over the remaining dressing.

"I'm not sure where I picked up my preference for anything topped with this spicy, creamy Buffalo sauce. But I'm sure happy I did."

grilled molasses-glazed chicken over pineapple slaw

This dish has a sticky sweetness and almost burnt-sugar flavor that comes from basting the chicken with a molasses-based glaze, then cooking it gently on the grill.

SERVES 4 PREP TIME 10 minutes COOK TIME 45 minutes

2 cups pineapple juice

3 tablespoons honey

4 tablespoons apple cider vinegar

¼ cup unsulphured molasses

¾ cup mayonnaise

½ cup chopped fresh pineapple with juice

1 (16-ounce/454-g) bag coleslaw mix

4 skinless, boneless chicken breast cutlets (about 1 pound/500 g)

Salt and pepper

1. In a medium saucepan, combine the pineapple juice, 2 tablespoons honey, 2 tablespoons vinegar and molasses; bring to a boil and simmer until thickened, about 30 minutes. Reserve about ½ cup of the glaze for drizzling.

2. Meanwhile, in a medium bowl, whisk together the mayonnaise, remaining 2 tablespoons vinegar and remaining 1 tablespoon honey; fold in the pineapple with juice. Add the coleslaw mix and toss to coat; refrigerate.

3. Preheat a grill or grill pan to medium heat. Season the chicken with salt and pepper and grill, turning once and basting occasionally with the glaze, until cooked through, about 15 minutes total. Let cool slightly; slice on a diagonal. Divide the slaw among four plates. Top each with sliced chicken and drizzle with the reserved glaze.

starters & salads

*"Sometimes I make this salad for a quick
weeknight dinner or as part of a brunch menu."*

warm fried shrimp salad
with chipotle bacon dressing

Technically this is a salad, but it's so much more. And it's rare to call a salad homey, but this one really is. The crispy fried shrimp wilt the greens ever so slightly, while the smoky bacon dressing pulls the dish together.

SERVES 4   PREP TIME 20 minutes   COOK TIME 25 minutes

½ cup Silvana's
All-Purpose Flour (page 15)

Salt

¾ cup plus 2 tablespoons
cold seltzer

1 cup vegetable oil, for frying

1 pound (500 g) medium
shrimp—peeled, deveined
and butterflied, with tails on

½ chipotle chile in
adobo sauce, seeded
and finely chopped

2 tablespoons ketchup

¼ cup mayonnaise

Juice of ½ lime

2 slices bacon, cooked
until crisp and crumbled

1 head red leaf
lettuce, chopped

1. In a large bowl, whisk together the flour and ¼ teaspoon salt. Add the seltzer and whisk until smooth.

2. In a large skillet, heat the oil over medium-high heat until shimmering. Working in batches, coat the shrimp with the batter, add to the hot oil and cook, turning once, until crisp, about 6 minutes total; drain on paper towels and sprinkle generously with salt. Repeat with the remaining shrimp and batter.

3. Meanwhile, in a small bowl, combine the chipotle, ketchup, mayonnaise, lime juice and bacon; season with salt.

4. In a large bowl, toss together the lettuce and dressing; top with the fried shrimp.

grilled shrimp salad with guacamole dressing and corn nuts

For even more creaminess, especially if your avocados aren't wonderfully ripe, add 1 tablespoon of mayonnaise to the dressing.

SERVES 4 **PREP TIME** 15 minutes **COOK TIME** 5 minutes

1 ripe Hass avocado—
halved, pitted and peeled

Juice of 1 lime

½ chipotle chile in adobo
sauce, seeded, or to taste

1 tablespoon chopped
fresh cilantro or parsley,
plus more for topping

Salt and pepper

½ cup water

¼ cup extra-virgin olive oil,
plus more for brushing

20 jumbo shrimp (about
1 pound/500 g), peeled and
deveined, with tails on

1 head iceberg lettuce,
quartered

Corn nuts, crushed,
for topping (optional)

1. In a food processor, combine the avocado, lime juice, chipotle, cilantro, ½ teaspoon salt and water; process until smooth. With the motor running, add the olive oil in a slow, steady stream; process until blended.

2. Preheat a grill or grill pan to medium-high heat. Brush the shrimp with olive oil and season with about ¼ teaspoon salt and ⅛ teaspoon pepper. Thread five shrimp crosswise on each of four skewers. Place on the grill, cover and cook, turning once, until the shrimp are firm and charred, about 5 minutes total. To serve, divide the lettuce among four plates. Top each wedge with a shrimp skewer and spoon over the guacamole dressing. Top with corn nuts, if using, and cilantro.

"One day for lunch, I was pulling leftovers out of the fridge. We'd had grilled shrimp the night before, and there was enough to make a salad. What I remember most from that lunch was that I wished I'd had more leftover shrimp— this salad is that good."

grilled corn and tomato salad with creamed corn dressing

When you cut the corn kernels off the cob, you'll be amazed at how much cream comes running down the knife. That's what gives this salad dressing its rich, creamed consistency. Mayonnaise and olive oil help, too. You can serve this refreshing salad at room temperature or cold from the fridge. For a quick summer supper, toss the salad with pasta or pile it on top of grilled fish or steak.

SERVES 4 **PREP TIME** 15 minutes **COOK TIME** 10 minutes

4 ears corn, husked

¼ cup extra-virgin olive oil, plus more for rubbing

2 tablespoons fresh lemon juice

1 tablespoon mayonnaise

Salt and pepper

2 cups cherry or grape tomatoes, halved

½ red onion, halved and thinly sliced

Finely grated zest of ½ lemon

½ cup fresh basil leaves, cut into thin strips

2 tablespoons chopped fresh tarragon

1. Preheat a grill or grill pan to medium-high heat. Rub the corn with olive oil and grill, turning occasionally, until tender and just charred, about 10 minutes. Let cool; cut the kernels off the cob.

2. In a food processor, combine ½ cup grilled corn kernels with the lemon juice and mayonnaise and pulse until coarsely chopped. With the motor running, add the olive oil in a slow, steady stream and process until blended; season with about ½ teaspoon salt and ¼ teaspoon pepper.

3. In a medium bowl, toss together the remaining grilled corn, tomatoes, onion, lemon zest and basil. Add the dressing and toss; top with the tarragon.

starters & salads

double-decker toasted cornbread and spicy greens stack

SERVES 4 **PREP TIME** 5 minutes

1 loaf Double Corn
Cornbread (see below)

2½ teaspoons sriracha
hot sauce, or to taste

2 tablespoons apple cider
vinegar

¾ teaspoon salt

1 teaspoon sugar

¼ cup extra-virgin olive oil

1 (5-ounce/150-g)
package mesclun

1. Cut the cornbread into eight slices, about ½ inch (1 cm) thick. Toast until golden.

2. In a large bowl, stir together the sriracha, vinegar, salt and sugar. Whisking continuously, add the olive oil in a slow, steady stream until blended. Add the greens and toss. To serve, arrange four slices of cornbread on four plates. Top with greens, another slice of cornbread and more greens.

double corn cornbread

SERVES 6 **PREP TIME** 10 minutes **COOK TIME** 45 minutes

1 cup rice milk

1 tablespoon apple cider vinegar

1 cup cornmeal, preferably
medium grind

1 cup Silvana's
All-Purpose Flour (page 15)

¼ cup sugar

1 tablespoon baking powder

1 teaspoon baking soda

1 teaspoon salt

2 large eggs, at room
temperature, lightly beaten

¼ cup vegetable oil

1 cup corn kernels
(about 1 ear corn)

1. Preheat the oven to 350°F. Grease a 4½-inch by 8½-inch (11-cm by 21-cm) loaf pan. In a small bowl, stir together the milk and vinegar. In a medium bowl, whisk together the cornmeal, flour, sugar, baking powder, baking soda and salt. Stir in the milk mixture, eggs and oil until just blended; fold in the corn kernels. Pour the batter into the prepared pan.

2. Bake until golden and a toothpick inserted in the center comes out clean, about 45 minutes. Let cool completely in the pan set on a wire rack.

starters & salads

grilled romaine with garlic caesar dressing and chickpea croutons

The warm, charred romaine works nicely with the cool, creamy dressing. If you have a big grill and it's too hot to turn on your oven, throw the chickpea croutons in a cast-iron skillet and cook, covered, until crisp. If you're short on time, serve the romaine uncooked or make the dressing ahead of time, cover and refrigerate for up to 3 days.

SERVES 4 PREP TIME 10 minutes COOK TIME 25 minutes

1 (15.5-ounce/540-mL) can chickpeas, rinsed and drained

4 tablespoons extra-virgin olive oil, plus more for rubbing

¼ teaspoon cayenne pepper

Salt and pepper

½ cup mayonnaise

1½ teaspoons Dijon mustard

½ teaspoon Worcestershire sauce

1 clove garlic, chopped

Finely grated zest and juice from ½ lemon

1 anchovy fillet (optional)

4 romaine hearts, halved lengthwise

1. Preheat the oven to 400°F. On a rimmed baking sheet, toss the chickpeas with 2 tablespoons olive oil, the cayenne, ½ teaspoon salt and ¼ teaspoon black pepper. Bake, shaking the pan occasionally, until golden and crisp, about 20 minutes.

2. Meanwhile, in a food processor, combine the mayonnaise, mustard, Worcestershire sauce, garlic, lemon juice, remaining 2 tablespoons olive oil and anchovy, if using; process until smooth.

3. Preheat a grill or grill pan to medium-high heat. Rub the romaine hearts with olive oil and season with about ¾ teaspoon salt and ¼ teaspoon pepper. Grill for about 3 minutes, turning occasionally, until slightly charred. Divide among four plates; drizzle with the dressing and top with the lemon zest and chickpea croutons.

arugula salad with bacon-walnut praline, pomegranate and apple cider vinaigrette

This praline delivers a sweet-salty fix—a hard habit to kick. You can make the praline up to 3 days in advance and store it, refrigerated, in a resealable plastic bag. Drizzle any leftover dressing over roasted vegetables or use it as a marinade for chicken.

SERVES 4 PREP TIME 15 minutes (plus cooling) COOK TIME 15 minutes

1 cup sugar

1 cup chopped walnuts

6 slices bacon, cooked until crisp and crumbled

1 cup apple cider

2 tablespoons apple cider vinegar

2 teaspoons whole-grain mustard

Salt and pepper

¼ cup extra-virgin olive oil

2 (5-ounce/150-g) packages arugula

½ cup pomegranate seeds

1. Line a baking sheet with parchment paper. In a large skillet, melt the sugar over medium-high heat until golden, about 7 minutes. Reduce the heat to low, add the walnuts and stir to coat. Transfer to the prepared baking sheet and spread in a single layer. Top with the bacon bits and let cool completely. Place the praline in a resealable plastic bag and crush into pieces.

2. In a small saucepan, boil the apple cider until slightly reduced, about 8 minutes. Whisk together with the vinegar, mustard, ½ teaspoon salt and ½ teaspoon pepper. Whisking continuously, add the olive oil in a slow, steady stream until blended. To serve, in a salad bowl, toss the arugula with the vinaigrette. Top with the pomegranate seeds and some of the bacon-walnut praline; save the rest of the praline for another use.

spinach and roasted vegetable salad with balsamic vinaigrette

The vinaigrette does double duty here, first as a marinade, then as the dressing. But it's how the warm roasted vegetables tenderly wilt the spinach leaves, coating them with all the delicious caramelized juices, that makes this salad irresistible.

SERVES 4 **PREP TIME** 20 minutes (plus cooling) **COOK TIME** 40 minutes

2 tablespoons balsamic vinegar

1 tablespoon Dijon mustard

1 clove garlic, smashed

⅓ cup extra-virgin olive oil

Salt and pepper

4 carrots, peeled and cut into ⅓-inch (0.8-cm) rounds

1 medium red onion, halved and sliced into thirds

2 bell peppers—halved, seeded and cut into ½-inch (1-cm) strips

2 zucchini, cut into ⅓-inch (0.8-cm) rounds

1 (6-ounce/175-g) bag baby spinach

Finely grated zest of 2 lemons

2 tablespoons chopped fresh parsley

1. Preheat the oven to 450°F. In a food processor, combine the vinegar, mustard and garlic; process until smooth. With the motor running, add the olive oil in a slow, steady stream; process until blended. Season with about ½ teaspoon salt and ¼ teaspoon pepper.

2. Place the carrots, onion, bell peppers and zucchini in a single layer on a rimmed baking sheet. Drizzle with some of the vinaigrette, reserving at least 2 tablespoons; toss to coat. Roast, stirring once, until tender, about 40 minutes. Let cool for at least 15 minutes. To serve, in a large bowl, toss together the spinach, lemon zest, parsley, roasted vegetables and reserved vinaigrette.

macaroni salad with sun-dried tomatoes and olives

This recipe holds on to those earthy Mediterranean flavors with the sun-dried tomatoes and oregano, but adds a little brininess with the olives. Sometimes toasted pine nuts or almonds are nice, too. You can prepare the salad a day ahead, then cover and refrigerate.

SERVES 4 **PREP TIME** 20 minutes (plus cooling) **COOK TIME** 25 minutes

2 cups corn or rice elbow macaroni

2 tablespoons extra-virgin olive oil, plus more for drizzling

½ cup chopped drained sun-dried tomatoes packed in olive oil

¼ cup chopped pitted black olives, such as Kalamata

2 stalks celery, finely chopped

1½ teaspoons Dijon mustard

¼ cup mayonnaise

1½ teaspoons fresh lemon juice

1 teaspoon chopped fresh oregano

½ teaspoon honey

¼ teaspoon salt

1. Bring a large pot of salted water to a boil. Add the macaroni, stirring to prevent sticking. Cook, partially covered, until al dente, about 14 minutes; rinse with cold water and drain. Spread evenly on a baking sheet, drizzle with olive oil and toss; let cool.

2. In a large bowl, combine the cooled macaroni, sun-dried tomatoes, olives and celery.

3. In a medium bowl, whisk together the mustard, mayonnaise, lemon juice, oregano, honey and salt. Whisking continuously, add the olive oil in a slow, steady stream until blended. Add the dressing to the macaroni mixture and toss.

potato salad with pickles and mustard vinaigrette

This potato salad is easy—and heat-friendly. Once you toss the warm potatoes with the pickles and vinaigrette, it's hard to keep your fingers out of the bowl, but the salad is even better cold from the fridge.

SERVES 4 **PREP TIME** 15 minutes (plus chilling) **COOK TIME** 15 minutes

2 pounds (1 kg) medium red potatoes, cut into 1-inch (2.5-cm) pieces

½ cup chopped sweet pickles

2 teaspoons Dijon mustard

2 tablespoons apple cider vinegar

2 tablespoons finely chopped red onion

2 tablespoons chopped fresh chives

¼ cup chopped fresh parsley

¼ cup extra-virgin olive oil

Salt and pepper

1. In a large pot of salted water, bring the potatoes to a boil over medium heat. Reduce the heat and simmer until fork-tender, about 10 minutes; drain. Place in a large bowl with the pickles.

2. In a small bowl, whisk together the mustard, vinegar, onion, chives and parsley. Whisking continuously, add the olive oil in a slow, steady stream until blended. Pour over the potatoes and toss gently; season with about ¾ teaspoon salt and ⅛ teaspoon pepper. Refrigerate until cold, about 1 hour.

soups, rice & pasta

I WENT TO THREE DIFFERENT SUPERMARKETS and bought all kinds of gluten-free pastas—white rice, brown rice with rice bran, corn, quinoa, buckwheat, millet and, yes, potato. I wasn't going to stop until I found pasta that both Isaiah and I liked. I had my Italian roots to live up to, after all. So I boiled up many different pastas until I found one we were happy with, not only for texture and flavor but also for how it held up the next day. Plenty of plates of pasta later, I realized that the trick to cooking any gluten-free pasta perfectly is to slightly undercook it since it will continue to cook once you toss it with sauce. Soups, on the other hand, are easy. I have lots of childhood memories of the smell of something simmering away on the stove, especially my mom's creamy tomato bisque. For Isaiah, it's my corn chowder. When the first chill breezes through the air, I start stuffing my pot full of vegetables and broth. After I clean up from breakfast, I chop onions and carrots or roast mushrooms for soup, then I let everything simmer, just as Mom did, until it's time for us to sit down to our cozy lunch.

"Isaiah was raised on pasta—and it's
one of my quick, convenient dinners."

"This soup tastes like my favorite part of chicken potpie—the rich filling of chicken and vegetables in a velvety-smooth sauce."

chicken potpie soup

Eggs, one of the original emulsifiers, give this soup its creamy consistency. If you've made custard before, you know that the trickiest step is tempering the eggs before you add them to the hot broth so the eggs don't curdle. Here's a foolproof method: Use your blender. First, blend the eggs; then, with the motor running, slowly stream in the broth.

SERVES 4 PREP TIME 10 minutes COOK TIME 45 minutes

2 tablespoons extra-virgin olive oil

1 small onion, finely chopped

2 stalks celery, cut into ¼-inch (0.5-cm) pieces

1 large carrot, peeled and cut into ¼-inch (0.5-cm) pieces

8 ounces (250 g) button mushrooms, sliced

4 sprigs thyme

8 cups chicken broth

½ cup long-grain white rice

2 large eggs, at room temperature

Shredded meat from 1 rotisserie chicken (about 2 cups), skin and bones discarded

½ cup frozen peas, thawed

Salt and pepper

Rippled potato chips, crumbled, for topping

Parsley, chopped, for topping

1. Heat the olive oil in a large pot over medium heat. Add the onion, celery and carrot, and cook until softened, about 5 minutes. Increase the heat to medium-high. Add the mushrooms and cook until softened, about 10 minutes. Add the thyme and broth; bring to a boil. Stir in the rice; reduce the heat to low, cover and simmer until the rice is cooked, about 20 minutes. Remove the soup from the heat; discard the thyme sprigs.

2. In a blender, beat the eggs. With the motor running, slowly stream in ½ cup broth from the soup. Return to the pot and cook over low heat, whisking, until the soup is slightly thickened, about 5 minutes. Add the chicken and peas, and cook until warmed through; season with about 1½ teaspoons salt and ¼ teaspoon pepper. Divide among four bowls and top with potato chips and parsley.

soups, rice & pasta

carrot-ginger bisque

Raw cashews are the secret to the creaminess that makes this soup a bisque. Lime is the other curious ingredient that transforms an otherwise ordinary carrot soup into something you'll crave.

SERVES 6 PREP TIME 15 minutes COOK TIME 40 minutes

2 tablespoons extra-virgin olive oil

1 onion, chopped

1 pound (500 g) carrots, chopped

1 cup raw cashews

1 (1-inch/2.5-cm) piece fresh ginger, peeled and grated

4 cups vegetable or chicken broth

1 cup rice milk

½ cup fresh cilantro or parsley, finely chopped

Juice of 1 to 2 limes

Salt

1. Heat the olive oil in a large pot over medium heat. Add the onion and cook until softened, about 5 minutes. Add the carrots, cashews, ginger and broth and bring to a boil. Simmer, covered, until the carrots are tender, 30 to 35 minutes. Stir in the milk and cilantro.

2. Using an immersion blender, puree until smooth. To serve, stir in the lime juice and season with about ½ teaspoon salt.

"Whenever my mom cooked up a can of Campbell's Tomato Bisque, it was code for comfort. Homemade is even better."

mom's tomato bisque

The bisque is thickened with cooked rice and then blended until creamy. The honey cuts the tomatoes' acidity and adds just a touch of sweetness.

SERVES 6   PREP TIME 5 minutes   COOK TIME 40 minutes

1 tablespoon extra-virgin olive oil

½ medium onion, chopped

2 carrots, chopped into small pieces

1 (28-ounce/796-mL) can diced tomatoes with juice

4 cups vegetable or chicken broth

½ cup cooked white rice

½ cup rice milk

1½ teaspoons honey

Salt and pepper

1. In a large pot, heat the olive oil over medium heat. Add the onion and carrots; cook, stirring occasionally, until softened, about 10 minutes. Reserve ¼ cup of the tomatoes and drain. Add the remaining tomatoes with their juice and the broth; cover and bring to a boil. Stir in the rice and simmer for 30 minutes.

2. Using an immersion blender, puree until smooth. Stir in the milk and honey; season with about ½ teaspoon salt and ¼ teaspoon pepper. Serve in shallow bowls; top each with some of the reserved tomatoes.

"I wanted a soup that tasted like spring in a bowl. I knew the only way to get that was to blanch the vegetables."

vegetable pesto soup

Until you've blanched a vegetable, it seems like a big deal, or at least fussy and time-consuming. This soup puts that myth to rest. Take the plunge, and just 15 minutes later you'll be sitting down to a satisfying spring soup.

SERVES 4 **PREP TIME** 15 minutes **COOK TIME** 15 minutes

5 tablespoons extra-virgin olive oil

1 small onion, finely chopped

2 cloves garlic, smashed

18 thin asparagus (about 8 ounces/250 g), trimmed and cut into ½-inch (1-cm) pieces

1 cup sugar snap peas, cut into ½-inch (1-cm) pieces

3 zucchini (about 1½ pounds/ 750 g), trimmed and cut into ½-inch (1-cm) pieces

4 cups loosely packed fresh basil leaves

1½ cups vegetable or chicken broth

Salt and pepper

1. In a medium saucepan, heat 1 tablespoon olive oil over medium-high heat. Add the onion and garlic; cook until softened, about 5 minutes.

2. Fill a large bowl with ice water. In a large pot of boiling water, blanch the asparagus, sugar snap peas and zucchini until fork-tender, about 5 minutes. Dunk into the prepared ice water bowl; drain and pat dry. Blanch the basil until bright green, about 45 seconds. Dunk into the prepared ice water bowl; drain and squeeze dry.

3. Place the onion mixture and half of the blanched vegetables and basil in a blender; process until smooth. With the motor running, drizzle in the remaining 4 tablespoons olive oil in a slow, steady stream.

4. Return the mixture to the pot and stir in the broth, remaining vegetables, 1 teaspoon salt and ½ teaspoon pepper; cook over medium heat until heated through, about 5 minutes.

"Isaiah wasn't much of a mushroom eater until he tried this bisque, which I had cooked as a light late supper for Stephen and me. I love when things like that happen."

roasted garlic–mushroom bisque with toasted hazelnuts

Add ½ cup more broth or water if you prefer your soup thinner.

SERVES 4 to 6 **PREP TIME** 20 minutes **COOK TIME** 40 minutes

20 ounces (625 g) button mushrooms, trimmed

½ large onion, quartered

3 cloves garlic, unpeeled

4 sprigs fresh rosemary

3 tablespoons extra-virgin olive oil

Salt and pepper

4 cups vegetable or chicken broth

1 small potato, peeled and cut into ½-inch (1-cm) pieces

¼ cup hazelnuts, chopped and toasted

1. Preheat the oven to 400°F. Place the mushrooms, onion, garlic and rosemary on a baking sheet. Drizzle with the olive oil and season with about ½ teaspoon each salt and pepper; toss to coat and spread out in a single layer. Roast, stirring occasionally, until tender, about 25 minutes; squeeze the garlic cloves from their skins.

2. Transfer the roasted vegetables to a large pot and add the broth and potato; bring to a boil over medium-high heat. Reduce the heat to medium and simmer until the potato is tender, about 15 minutes; remove and discard the rosemary. Working in batches, transfer the soup to a blender and puree; return to the pot and reheat. Ladle into bowls and top with the toasted hazelnuts.

tomato-lime black bean soup with avocado cream

With the black beans, this soup is more or less a meal.

SERVES 6 **PREP TIME** 20 minutes **COOK TIME** 1 hour 15 minutes

2 tablespoons extra-virgin olive oil

1 medium onion, finely chopped

2 cloves garlic, smashed

1 teaspoon packed light brown sugar

2 (15-ounce/540-mL) cans black beans, rinsed and drained

4 cups vegetable or chicken broth

1 (28-ounce/796-mL) can diced fire-roasted tomatoes with juice

2 jalapeño peppers, stemmed and seeded

1 chipotle chile in adobo sauce, or to taste

½ cup loosely packed finely chopped fresh cilantro, plus more for serving

4 tablespoons lime juice (about 3 limes)

Salt

1 ripe avocado, peeled and pitted

1. In a soup pot, heat the olive oil over medium heat. Add the onion, garlic and brown sugar and cook until the onion is translucent and caramelized, about 10 minutes. Add the beans and broth; bring to a boil. Reduce the heat and cook until the beans fall apart, stirring occasionally, about 45 minutes.

2. Add the tomatoes and simmer for 15 minutes. Remove 2 cups of the soup and puree with the jalapeños, chipotle and cilantro; return to the pot. Stir in 2 tablespoons of the lime juice and season with about 1 teaspoon salt.

3. Meanwhile, place the avocado and the remaining 2 tablespoons lime juice in a food processor and process until creamy; season with about ½ teaspoon salt. To serve, top the soup with the avocado cream and cilantro.

creamy corn chowder

Cannellini beans may not be among the most commonly used ingredients in corn chowder, but they give this soup an undeniably creamy, comforting consistency.

SERVES 4 PREP TIME 12 minutes COOK TIME 20 minutes

2 tablespoons extra-virgin olive oil

1 small onion, finely chopped

2 stalks celery, cut into ¼-inch (0.5-cm) pieces

1 potato, peeled and cut into ½-inch (1-cm) pieces

4 ears corn, kernels removed

1 (15-ounce/540-mL) can cannellini beans—drained, rinsed and mashed until creamy

4 cups vegetable or chicken broth

Salt

¼ teaspoon cayenne pepper, plus more for sprinkling

Fresh chives, chopped, for topping

In a large pot, heat 2 tablespoons olive oil over medium-high heat. Add the onion and celery; cook until softened, about 5 minutes. Add the potato, three-quarters of the corn kernels, the beans and broth; bring to a boil. Reduce the heat to medium and simmer until the potato is tender, about 15 minutes; season with about 2 teaspoons salt and the cayenne pepper. Divide the soup among four bowls and top with the remaining corn kernels, chives and a sprinkling of cayenne.

"The first summer I made chowder with just-picked corn, Isaiah was hooked. He kept asking for more, but we had already finished the chowder, so he licked the ladle."

loaded baked potato chowder

Leave it to a baked potato to lend inspiration for chowder. For the creamiest consistency, use a potato ricer. You can also run the potatoes through a food mill or sieve.

SERVES 4 to 6 PREP TIME 15 minutes COOK TIME 1 hour 30 minutes

3 russet potatoes
(about 2 pounds/1 kg total)

Extra-virgin olive oil,
for rubbing

Salt and pepper

4 slices bacon

1 small onion, chopped

2 stalks celery, chopped

4 cups chicken broth

1 cup rice milk

2 tablespoons finely chopped
chives, for topping

1. Preheat the oven to 400°F. Using a fork, poke the potatoes in a few places, then rub with olive oil and sprinkle with about ½ teaspoon salt; bake until crispy on the outside and creamy on the inside, about 1 hour. Let cool slightly, then halve lengthwise and scoop out the flesh; put the flesh through a potato ricer and discard the skins.

2. Meanwhile, in a large pot over medium heat, cook the bacon, turning once, until crisp and the fat has rendered, about 10 minutes. Remove the bacon and drain on paper towels; crumble.

3. Add the onion and celery to the bacon fat and cook until softened, about 5 minutes. Stir in the broth and milk; bring to a boil. Stir in the potatoes and cook, stirring occasionally, until heated through, about 5 minutes.

4. Using an immersion blender, puree the soup until smooth; season with about ½ teaspoon salt and ¼ teaspoon pepper. Ladle into shallow bowls and top with the bacon bits and chives.

"I have a thing for Stouffer's Turkey Tetrazzini. It dates back to my childhood when my father traveled for work and my mom would pull out the Stouffer's from the freezer."

chicken rice tetrazzini with mushroom gravy and mustard crumbs

You can substitute more milk or water for the white wine.

SERVES 4 **PREP TIME** 10 minutes **COOK TIME** 45 minutes

1 cup rice cereal crumbs

1 tablespoon Dijon mustard

3 tablespoons chopped fresh parsley

2 tablespoons extra-virgin olive oil, plus more for drizzling

20 ounces (625 g) button mushrooms, sliced

2 tablespoons Silvana's All-Purpose Flour (page 15)

½ cup white wine

½ cup rice milk

2 cups water

Salt and pepper

1 cup long-grain rice

2 packed cups chopped rotisserie chicken

1. Preheat the oven to 350°F. Grease a 9-inch by 13-inch (22.5-cm by 32.5-cm) baking dish. In a small bowl, combine the cereal crumbs, mustard and 1 tablespoon parsley.

2. In a large skillet, heat the olive oil over medium-high heat. Add the mushrooms and cook, stirring occasionally, until softened, about 5 minutes. Sprinkle the flour on top; stir for 1 minute. Stir in the wine and milk and simmer, stirring occasionally, until slightly thickened, about 3 minutes. Stir in the water, the remaining 2 tablespoons parsley, 1½ teaspoons salt and ½ teaspoon pepper.

3. Spread the uncooked rice in an even layer in the prepared baking dish; top with the chicken. Pour the mushroom gravy on top. Cover snugly with aluminum foil and bake until bubbly, about 30 minutes. Remove the casserole from the oven, sprinkle the mustard crumbs on top and drizzle with olive oil; bake for 5 minutes more.

"I've stirred my fair share of pots full of simmering risotto. No more. Now I let the oven do all the work for me."

asparagus risotto casserole

Like all risottos, this recipe is easily adapted to whatever vegetables you have on hand. Before serving, stir in fresh herbs and lemon zest to wake up the flavors.

SERVES 4 to 6   PREP TIME 15 minutes   COOK TIME 40 minutes

2 tablespoons extra-virgin olive oil

½ onion, finely chopped

2 cloves garlic, finely chopped

2 cups Arborio rice

Salt and pepper

¼ cup white wine

4 cups vegetable or chicken broth

1 cup water

1 pound (500 g) thin asparagus, trimmed and cut into 1½-inch (3.5-cm) pieces

1 cup loosely packed fresh flat-leaf parsley, finely chopped

Finely grated zest of 1 lemon

1. Preheat the oven to 375°F. In a heavy ovenproof pot, heat the olive oil over medium heat. Add the onion and cook until softened, about 4 minutes. Add the garlic and rice; season with about 1½ teaspoons salt and ½ teaspoon pepper. Cook, stirring, until the rice is toasted, about 3 minutes. Stir in the wine and cook for 1 minute. Stir in the broth and water; bake, uncovered, for 35 minutes.

2. Remove the risotto from the oven and stir in the asparagus. Continue to bake, uncovered, until the rice is tender, about 5 minutes more. Stir in the parsley and lemon zest.

butternut squash rice bake with toasted hazelnut–sage crunch

The flavor combinations in this rice bake may be Italian in nature, but the method is all-American. The dish is great for entertaining, particularly with the simple but elegant crunchy hazelnut–sage topping.

SERVES 4 PREP TIME 10 minutes COOK TIME 55 minutes

**1 butternut squash
(about 3 pounds/1½ kg),
peeled and cut into ½-inch
(1-cm) pieces**

**4 tablespoons extra-virgin
olive oil, plus more for
drizzling**

Salt and pepper

½ cup rice cereal crumbs

½ cup hazelnuts, chopped

**1½ teaspoons finely chopped
fresh sage**

2 cloves garlic, finely chopped

2 cups Arborio rice

**4 cups vegetable or
chicken broth**

1¼ cups water

1. Preheat the oven to 450°F. Place the squash on a baking sheet and toss with 2 tablespoons olive oil; season generously with about 1 teaspoon salt and ¼ teaspoon pepper and spread out in a single layer. Roast until golden and tender, turning once, about 20 minutes; remove from the oven. Reduce the oven temperature to 375°F.

2. In a small bowl, combine the cereal crumbs, hazelnuts, sage and ¼ teaspoon salt.

3. In a heavy ovenproof pot, heat the remaining 2 tablespoons olive oil over medium heat. Add the garlic and cook until golden, about 2 minutes. Add the rice; season with 1½ teaspoons salt and ¼ teaspoon pepper. Cook, stirring, until the rice is toasted, about 3 minutes. Stir in the broth and water; bake, uncovered, for 25 minutes. Remove the risotto from the oven and stir in the squash. Continue to bake, uncovered, until the rice is tender, about 5 minutes more.

4. Preheat the broiler. Top the rice with the hazelnut crumbs and drizzle with olive oil; broil until crunchy and golden, about 3 minutes.

pan-fried shrimp and caramelized scallion rice cakes

You can keep the rice cakes warm in a 200°F oven or just cover loosely with foil.

MAKES 8 rice cakes **PREP TIME** 10 minutes (plus chilling) **COOK TIME** 1 hour

5 tablespoons extra-virgin olive oil

6 scallions, trimmed and coarsely chopped

1 tablespoon sugar

2 tablespoons balsamic vinegar

1 cup Arborio rice

2 cups vegetable or chicken broth

½ cup water

8 ounces (250 g) medium shrimp—peeled, deveined and cut into ¼-inch (0.5-cm) pieces

1 teaspoon hot sauce, such as Tabasco, or to taste

Salt and pepper

2 large eggs, lightly beaten

1. Preheat the oven to 375°F. In a small ovenproof pot, heat 1 tablespoon olive oil over medium heat. Add the scallions and sugar and cook, stirring occasionally, until caramelized, about 10 minutes; stir in the vinegar and let cook for 1 minute. Transfer to a plate.

2. Wipe out the pot and heat 2 tablespoons olive oil over medium heat. Add the rice and cook, stirring, until the rice is toasted, about 3 minutes. Stir in the broth and water; bake, uncovered, for 30 minutes. Remove the risotto from the oven and stir in the scallions, shrimp, hot sauce, 1 teaspoon salt and ½ teaspoon pepper; let cool to room temperature. Stir in the eggs and refrigerate for about 1 hour.

3. Shape the rice mixture into eight cakes, each about ½ inch (1 cm) thick. Refrigerate for about 1 hour.

4. In a large skillet, heat 1 tablespoon olive oil over medium-high heat. Add four rice cakes and cook undisturbed, turning once, until golden and firm to the touch, about 8 minutes total. Drain on paper towels. Repeat with the remaining 1 tablespoon olive oil and rice cakes.

*"It doesn't take much—15 minutes, to be exact—
to get this creamy, rich dish in the oven."*

portobello-rice quiche

For more garlic flavor, finely chop the garlic before cooking it in the olive oil. If you
don't have a pie shell, you can make an instant crumb crust. Just lightly grease the
bottom and sides of a baking pan, then sprinkle rice cereal crumbs all over to cover.

SERVES 6 **PREP TIME** 15 minutes (plus cooling) **COOK TIME** 1 hour

2 tablespoons extra-virgin olive oil

3 cloves garlic, smashed

12 ounces (375 g) portobello mushrooms (about 6)— half cut into ½-inch (1-cm) pieces and half sliced about ¼ inch (0.5 cm) thick

Salt

6 large eggs

1 cup rice milk

2 tablespoons finely chopped fresh parsley, plus more for sprinkling

¾ cup cooked long-grain rice

1 baked All-Purpose Pie Crust (page 213) or 1 store-bought baked 9-inch (23-cm) pie shell, brushed with 1 beaten egg white

1. Preheat the oven to 400°F. In a skillet, heat 1 tablespoon olive oil over medium heat. Add the garlic and cook until golden, about 1 minute. Add the mushroom pieces and cook until the liquid evaporates, about 5 minutes; transfer to a plate.

2. In the same skillet, heat the remaining 1 tablespoon olive oil; cook the mushroom slices until golden, about 8 minutes. Remove from the heat and season with about ⅛ teaspoon salt.

3. In a large bowl, whisk together the eggs, milk, parsley and 1 teaspoon salt; fold in the rice and garlic-mushroom mixture. Pour into the baked pie shell and bake for 25 minutes. Top with the mushroom slices and sprinkle with parsley; bake until set and golden around the edges, about 20 minutes more. Let cool in the pan set on a wire rack for 15 minutes before serving.

minestrone rigatoni with bacon chips

If the bacon doesn't render enough fat, add olive oil.

SERVES 4 **PREP TIME** 25 minutes **COOK TIME** 20 minutes

6 slices bacon, halved crosswise

1 small onion, finely chopped

3½ cups water

Salt and pepper

8 ounces (250 g) corn or rice rigatoni

1 (15-ounce/540-mL) can cannellini beans, rinsed and drained

2 zucchini (about 1 pound/ 500 g), cut into matchsticks

1 cup fresh or frozen peas, thawed

2 tablespoons chopped fresh basil

2 tablespoons chopped fresh parsley

1 teaspoon chopped fresh mint

2 teaspoons finely grated lemon zest

1. In a large skillet, cook the bacon over medium heat until crisp, about 10 minutes. Reserve 2 tablespoons of the fat and drain the bacon on paper towels.

2. In a large saucepan, heat the reserved bacon fat over medium heat. Add the onion and cook until softened, about 5 minutes. Add the water and 1 teaspoon salt and bring to a boil. Stir in the pasta and simmer, stirring frequently, until the pasta is just tender, about 8 minutes. Stir in the beans, zucchini and peas; season with about ¼ teaspoon each salt and pepper. Return to a simmer and cook, stirring occasionally, until fork-tender, about 4 minutes. Remove from the heat and stir in the basil, parsley, mint and lemon zest. Using a slotted spoon, transfer the pasta and vegetables to bowls. Top with the bacon chips.

soups, rice & pasta

spaghetti and meatballs with garlic crumbs

There's no question—if you make spaghetti and meatballs, the kids will eat it. The garlic crumbs add a nice crunch.

SERVES 4 **PREP TIME** 15 minutes **COOK TIME** 40 minutes

1 pound (500 g) ground beef chuck

1 small onion, grated

5 cloves garlic—2 grated, 2 smashed and 1 chopped

1 cup rice cereal crumbs

½ cup rice milk

1 large egg

6 tablespoons chopped flat-leaf parsley

Salt

2 tablespoons extra-virgin olive oil

2 (28-ounce/796-mL) cans crushed tomatoes

1 (12-ounce/375-g) package corn or rice spaghetti

½ teaspoon crushed red pepper flakes, or to taste

1. In a large bowl, combine the beef, onion, chopped garlic, ½ cup cereal crumbs, milk, egg, 2 tablespoons parsley and 1 teaspoon salt; shape into eight 2-inch (5-cm) balls.

2. In a large saucepan, heat 1 tablespoon olive oil over medium heat. Add the smashed garlic and cook until golden, about 2 minutes. Add the tomatoes and bring to a simmer, stirring occasionally. Submerge the meatballs in the sauce; bring to a simmer and cook, covered and stirring occasionally, for 20 minutes. Season with about 1 teaspoon salt.

3. In a large pot of boiling salted water, cook the spaghetti until al dente, about 15 minutes; drain and toss with the sauce.

4. To make the garlic crumbs, heat the remaining 1 tablespoon olive oil in a small skillet over medium heat. Add the grated garlic, remaining ½ cup cereal crumbs, red pepper flakes and ¼ teaspoon salt. Cook until toasted, 1 to 2 minutes. Let cool, then stir in the remaining 4 tablespoons parsley. To serve, divide the spaghetti among shallow bowls and top with meatballs and garlic crumbs.

pumpkin dumplings with bacon and radicchio

Something to keep in mind when you make this recipe—it's a lot easier than you think. The dumplings are superlight and pillowy, but if you prefer a firmer texture, add more flour, 1 tablespoon at a time, to the pasta dough.

SERVES 4   PREP TIME 25 minutes   COOK TIME 20 minutes

1 (15-ounce/540-mL) can
pure pumpkin puree

2 large eggs, lightly beaten

1 cup Silvana's
All-Purpose Flour (page 15)

Salt

4 ounces (about 6 slices)
thick-sliced bacon, chopped

1 medium onion,
finely chopped

¼ teaspoon crushed
red pepper flakes

1 small head radicchio,
sliced into ¼-inch (0.5-cm)
strips (about 2 cups)

2 tablespoons chopped
fresh flat-leaf parsley

1. Bring a large pot of salted water to a boil. In a large bowl, combine the pumpkin puree, eggs, flour and 1 teaspoon salt.

2. In a large saucepan, cook the bacon over medium heat until crispy, about 15 minutes. Add the onion and red pepper flakes and cook until softened, about 5 minutes; remove from the heat.

3. When the water comes to a boil, use a teaspoon to scoop the dough, then carefully slide the dumpling off the spoon and into the boiling water. Continue forming dumplings until half the dough is used. Cook until the dumplings float, then simmer for about 2 minutes; remove with a slotted spoon and add to the saucepan with the bacon. Repeat with the remaining dumpling dough.

4. Return the saucepan with the bacon to medium-high heat. Toss in three-quarters of the radicchio and stir gently until just wilted, about 2 minutes; season with about ½ teaspoon salt. To serve, divide the dumplings and sauce among four bowls and top with the remaining radicchio and parsley.

1 Mix together the pasta dough.

2 Shape the dough into ovals with two spoons.

3 Slide the dough off the spoon and into the boiling water.

fusilli with sun-dried tomato sauce

Sun-dried tomatoes can be bitter, but not if you counterbalance them with ginger and lemon. If the sauce thickens too much, just add pasta cooking water, 1 tablespoon at a time, until you get the consistency you want.

SERVES 4   PREP TIME 5 minutes   COOK TIME 15 minutes

1 pound (500 g) corn or rice fusilli pasta or other short pasta

1 (14.5-ounce/398-mL) can chopped tomatoes with juice

¼ cup drained oil-packed sun-dried tomatoes

1 tablespoon fresh lemon juice

1 clove garlic

1 teaspoon grated fresh ginger

1 teaspoon salt

¼ cup extra-virgin olive oil

Basil leaves, torn, for serving

1. In a large pot of boiling salted water, cook the pasta until al dente, about 15 minutes; drain and return to the pot.

2. Meanwhile, in a food processor, combine the chopped tomatoes with their juice, sun-dried tomatoes, lemon juice, garlic, ginger and salt; process until smooth. With the motor running, add the olive oil in a slow, steady stream until smooth. Stir the tomato sauce into the pasta and toss; top with basil.

penne with walnut cream sauce

You can grind nuts into nut butter, but that won't make a pasta sauce. If you soften nuts before processing them, they turn creamy, not oily. They also soak up a lot of liquid. If your sauce thickens, add more water and season with salt. Any leftover sauce keeps, covered, in the refrigerator for up to 3 days. Use it as a pizza sauce or spoon it over roasted vegetables.

SERVES 4 PREP TIME 10 minutes COOK TIME 30 minutes

2¼ cups walnuts, ¼ cup toasted for topping

1 clove garlic, peeled

¼ teaspoon ground nutmeg

¼ teaspoon crushed red pepper flakes

Salt and pepper

½ cup extra-virgin olive oil

1 pound (500 g) corn or rice penne or other short pasta

2 tablespoons finely chopped fresh parsley

1. Bring a large pot of salted water to a boil. Add the walnuts and garlic and cook until tender, about 15 minutes.

2. Using a slotted spoon, transfer the walnuts and garlic to a food processor and reserve 1¼ cups cooking water. Add the nutmeg, crushed red pepper, ½ teaspoon salt, ⅛ teaspoon black pepper and about 1¼ cups reserved cooking water to the food processor; process until finely chopped, about 30 seconds. With the motor running, stream in the olive oil and process until creamy, about 5 minutes; transfer to a serving bowl.

3. Meanwhile, add the pasta to the large pot of boiling salted water and cook until al dente; drain and toss with the sauce. To serve, divide the pasta among four shallow bowls and top with the toasted walnuts and parsley.

"Before this recipe, I had never blanched a nut in my life — oh, the difference a day makes."

sandwiches & pizza

I'M NOT GONNA LIE. Sure, Isaiah can go to a restaurant and order off the menu. But sometimes he just wants that slice of pizza. Or there's nothing he wants more than to bite into a sandwich. It's not always easy. That's where this chapter comes in. It makes everything easy again. You won't miss the bread. You won't miss the cheese. Originally, this chapter didn't exist. I didn't think I could pull it off to satisfy my own expectations, let alone Isaiah's. You don't know how many store-bought gluten-free breads, rolls and bagels I've had to toss in the garbage. They would fall apart before Isaiah even had the chance to take out his sandwich at lunchtime. They had an off flavor. They didn't look or behave like bread we knew and loved. Those breads were dense and crumbly; I wanted crusty and airy. So I started experimenting. I read all of the ingredient labels so I knew what I didn't want to use in my recipes. I even tried a bread machine once—that was my first and last time. I couldn't figure it out. At the same time, I was working on pizza dough, and I knew that the best dough would be one that could be used for both pizza and bread. That was the beginning of the messy, floury realization that the smaller the end product—a small pizza or a roll—the better the outcome. And I knew I was onto something when I hijacked my waffle iron to cook up savory waffles that I could swap for classic sandwich bread. Not only was it fun, but Isaiah couldn't be happier eating a waffle sandwich for lunch.

"Pizza has been a constant in our
lives since we discovered the
deliciously convenient New York
slice. Now we can bake our own
pizza and eat it hot from the oven."

"I started making savory waffles one day and never looked back. They're fast. They're easy. They're fun!"

meatloaf sandwiches on sun-dried tomato waffle bread

There may be quite a list of ingredients below. That's what happens with meatloaf—at least one that's moist and full of flavor.

SERVES 4 **PREP TIME** 25 minutes **COOK TIME** 1 hour 16 minutes

meatloaf

2 tablespoons extra-virgin olive oil

1 small onion, chopped

1 carrot, grated

1 clove garlic, grated

2 pounds (1 kg) ground beef

¾ cup ketchup

2 large eggs, lightly beaten

1 cup rice cereal crumbs

1 tablespoon finely chopped fresh parsley

1 tablespoon finely chopped fresh oregano

Salt and pepper

waffle bread

2 cups Silvana's Pancake Mix (page 15)

½ cup drained and chopped oil-packed sun-dried tomatoes

½ teaspoon salt

2 large eggs, at room temperature, lightly beaten

¼ cup vegetable oil

1½ cups rice milk

Italian seasoning blend

Sliced tomatoes, for serving

4 iceberg lettuce leaves, for serving

Mayonnaise, for serving

1. Preheat the oven to 350°F. Grease a 5-inch by 9-inch (12.5-cm by 22.5-cm) loaf pan. To make the meatloaf, in a skillet, heat the olive oil over medium heat. Add the onion and carrot and cook until softened, about 5 minutes. Add the garlic and cook about 1 minute. Let cool.

2. In a medium bowl, combine the beef, ½ cup ketchup, eggs, cereal crumbs, onion mixture, parsley, oregano, 2 teaspoons salt and 1 teaspoon pepper. Transfer to the prepared pan, rounding the top. Spread the remaining ¼ cup ketchup on top. Bake until cooked through, about 1 hour. Let set for about 10 minutes; cut into ½-inch (1-cm) slices.

3. To make the waffle bread, in a large bowl, whisk together the pancake mix, sun-dried tomatoes and salt. In a small bowl, whisk together the eggs, oil and milk. Add to the pancake mix mixture and stir until just combined.

4. Preheat a waffle iron to medium-high heat. Grease the waffle iron with nonstick cooking spray. Pour about ⅓ cup batter into each waffle iron square, spreading the batter out to the edges, and sprinkle with the Italian seasoning blend. Close and cook until crisp, about 5 minutes; let cool. Repeat with the remaining batter.

5. To assemble, top four waffles with tomato slices, a lettuce leaf, a meatloaf slice, mayonnaise and another waffle.

sandwiches & pizza

egg salad remoulade on everything waffle bread

Having a freezer full of waffle bread comes in handy. Transfer to the refrigerator to defrost overnight or microwave on high for 15-second intervals until softened, then toast.

SERVES 4 PREP TIME 20 minutes COOK TIME 25 minutes

waffle bread

2 tablespoons dry minced garlic

2 tablespoons dry minced onion

2 teaspoons sesame seeds

2 teaspoons poppy seeds

Salt

2 cups Silvana's Pancake Mix (page 15)

2 large eggs, at room temperature, lightly beaten

¼ cup vegetable oil

1½ cups rice milk

egg salad

10 large eggs, at room temperature

½ cup mayonnaise

1 tablespoon Dijon mustard

1 teaspoon fresh lemon juice

3 tablespoons finely chopped sweet gherkins

2 teaspoons finely chopped fresh parsley

½ teaspoon paprika

Salt and pepper

1. To make the waffle bread, in a small bowl, stir together the garlic, onion, sesame seeds, poppy seeds and 1 teaspoon salt.

2. Preheat a waffle iron to medium-high heat. In a large bowl, whisk together the pancake mix and ½ teaspoon salt.

3. In a small bowl, whisk together the eggs, oil and milk. Add to the pancake mix mixture and stir until just combined. Grease the waffle iron with nonstick cooking spray. Pour about ⅓ cup batter into each waffle iron square, spreading the batter out to the edges, and sprinkle generously with the seasoning mixture. Close and cook until crisp, about 5 minutes; let cool. Repeat with the remaining batter.

4. To make the egg salad, in a medium saucepan, combine the eggs and enough water to cover by 1 inch (2.5 cm). Bring to a boil, remove from the heat, cover and let stand for 15 minutes; drain. Place in a large bowl with cold water and let cool.

5. Peel the eggs and place in a medium bowl. Add the mayonnaise, mustard and lemon juice; mash to combine. Stir in the gherkins and parsley; season with the paprika, about ½ teaspoon salt and ¼ teaspoon pepper.

6. To assemble, sandwich a quarter of the egg salad between two waffles; repeat with the remaining egg salad and waffles. To serve, cut in half diagonally.

griddled banana bread sandwiches with nut butter, bacon and honey

You can make the banana bread up to 3 days ahead of time.

SERVES 4   PREP TIME 10 minutes   COOK TIME 3 minutes

8 (¼-inch/0.5-cm) slices
Mom's Banana Bread
(see below), toasted

½ cup peanut butter
or almond butter

1 ripe banana, cut into
¼-inch (0.5-cm) slices

Honey, for drizzling

8 slices bacon, cooked until crisp

1 tablespoon vegetable oil

1. Spread each slice of bread with 1 tablespoon peanut butter. Top four slices with a quarter of the banana slices, a drizzle of honey, two bacon slices and another bread slice, peanut butter side down.

2. In a nonstick skillet, heat the oil over medium heat. Add the sandwiches to the skillet and cook, turning once, until golden and crisp, about 3 minutes. To serve, cut in half diagonally.

mom's banana bread

MAKES 1 loaf   PREP TIME 5 minutes   COOK TIME 50 minutes

1¼ cups Silvana's
All-Purpose Flour (page 15)

2 teaspoons baking powder

1½ teaspoons ground cinnamon

½ teaspoon salt

2 large eggs, at room
temperature

1 cup sugar

1¼ cups mashed bananas
(about 3 ripe bananas)

2 teaspoons pure vanilla extract

½ cup vegetable oil

1. Preheat the oven to 350°F. Grease an 8½-inch by 4½-inch (21-cm by 11-cm) loaf pan with nonstick cooking spray. In a large bowl, whisk together the flour, baking powder, cinnamon and salt.

2. In a small bowl, whisk together the eggs, sugar, bananas, vanilla and oil. Stir the wet ingredients into the dry until just combined. Transfer the batter to the prepared pan. Bake until golden and a toothpick inserted in the center comes out dry, about 50 minutes. Let cool completely in the pan set on a wire rack.

toasted ham-and-tomato cornbread sandwiches with jalapeño mayonnaise

The jalapeño mayonnaise delivers a little kick and keeps the cornbread moist. If you're using my cornbread recipe (page 75), bake the cornbread in an 8-inch (20-cm) square baking pan for 35 to 40 minutes.

SERVES 4 **PREP TIME** 15 minutes

½ cup mayonnaise

3 jalapeños, seeded and chopped

¼ cup fresh cilantro or parsley leaves

1 tablespoon fresh lime juice

1 teaspoon honey

¼ teaspoon ground cumin

Salt

4 (4-inch/10-cm) squares Double Corn Cornbread (page 75) or store-bought cornbread, split and toasted

Shredded lettuce (about 2 cups), for topping

1 pound (500 g) deli-sliced smoked ham

4 tomato slices, for topping

1. In a food processor, combine the mayonnaise, jalapeños, cilantro, lime juice, honey, cumin and ¼ teaspoon salt. Process until smooth.

2. Spread about 1 tablespoon of the jalapeño mayonnaise on each cornbread bottom; top each with shredded lettuce, ham and a tomato slice. Spread the remaining jalapeño mayonnaise on each cornbread top and set in place. To serve, cut in half diagonally.

"Isaiah could eat cornbread for breakfast, lunch and dinner. Here, I sandwich ham and tomato between slices of buttery cornbread."

bread slabs

You can split and freeze the baked bread slabs for up to 1 month. To defrost, transfer to the refrigerator overnight or microwave for 15-second intervals until softened, then toast.

MAKES 4 bread slabs PREP TIME 5 minutes (plus resting) COOK TIME 10 minutes

2 cups Silvana's All-Purpose Flour (page 15), plus more for dusting

1 (¼-ounce/7.5-g) package active dry yeast

1 teaspoon salt, plus more for sprinkling

1 teaspoon sugar

2 large egg whites, at room temperature, lightly beaten

2 tablespoons extra-virgin olive oil, plus more for brushing

¾ cup warm water

1. In a large bowl, whisk together the flour, yeast, salt and sugar. Add the egg whites, olive oil and water. Using a wooden spoon, beat until the dough pulls away from the sides of the bowl.

2. Turn the dough onto a lightly floured, 12-inch (30-cm)-long piece of parchment paper. Lightly flour the top and, using your fingertips or a rolling pin, press the dough to form a rectangle about ¾ inch (1.5 cm) thick. Cover loosely with plastic wrap and let rest at room temperature for about 30 minutes. Cut into four equal pieces.

3. Position a rack in the bottom of the oven with a baking stone on the rack and preheat to 450°F. Brush each dough piece with olive oil and sprinkle with salt. Slide the dough pieces with parchment paper onto the preheated baking stone and bake until puffy and crisp on the bottom, about 10 minutes. Let cool on a wire rack.

VARIATIONS

chocolate chip bread slabs

Mix the dough as above. Gently stir in ¼ cup mini chocolate chips, being careful not to overmix to avoid melting. Proceed as above.

olive-oregano bread slabs

Mix the dough as above. Stir in ½ cup pitted, coarsely chopped mixed olives and 1½ teaspoons dried oregano. Proceed as above.

"Nutella was a standard sandwich filling in my lunchbox. Then one day I made it myself— there's nothing like the real deal."

chocolate-hazelnut butter on toasted chocolate chip bread slabs

To roast the hazelnuts, preheat the oven to 325°F and place them in a single layer on a baking sheet. Cook, shaking occasionally, until toasted and fragrant, about 12 minutes, and let cool completely. The chocolate-hazelnut butter will keep for about 1 month in the refrigerator.

SERVES 4 **PREP TIME** 6 minutes

2 cups blanched hazelnuts, roasted

¼ cup unsweetened cocoa powder, sifted

½ cup confectioners' sugar, sifted

1 teaspoon pure vanilla extract

⅛ teaspoon salt

3½ tablespoons vegetable oil

4 Chocolate Chip Bread Slabs (opposite page) or store-bought rolls, split and toasted

1. In a food processor, grind the hazelnuts, scraping down the sides, until smooth, about 2 minutes. Add the cocoa powder, confectioners' sugar, vanilla, salt and oil; process until combined, about 3 minutes.

2. To assemble, spread some of the chocolate-hazelnut butter on each bread bottom; set the bread tops in place. To serve, cut in half diagonally.

hummus, roasted tomato and pine nuts on olive-oregano bread slabs

This sandwich has a lot of flavors going on. It's salty, briny and even sweet—all in one bite. You can make the hummus ahead of time and refrigerate it, covered, for up to 2 days.

SERVES 4   PREP TIME 15 minutes   COOK TIME 28 minutes

2 cups grape tomatoes

¼ cup extra-virgin olive oil, plus more for drizzling

Salt and pepper

4 cloves garlic, unpeeled

1 (15-ounce/540-mL) can chickpeas, drained and rinsed

2 tablespoons tahini

Juice of 2 lemons

2 tablespoons water

4 Olive-Oregano Bread Slabs (page 116) or store-bought rolls, split and toasted

Paprika, for sprinkling

Fresh parsley, chopped, for topping

Pine nuts, toasted, for topping

1. Preheat the oven to 400°F. Place the tomatoes on a baking sheet, generously drizzle with olive oil and season with salt and pepper; toss. Spread into a single layer and roast, shaking the baking sheet once, until shriveled, about 20 minutes.

2. Meanwhile, in a small saucepan of boiling salted water, cook the garlic until softened, about 8 minutes. Let cool slightly and squeeze the garlic cloves from their skins.

3. In a food processor, combine the chickpeas, olive oil, tahini, lemon juice, garlic and water; process until creamy, about 2 minutes. Season with about ½ teaspoon salt.

4. To assemble, spread some of the hummus on the bread bottom, and sprinkle with paprika. Top with the roasted tomatoes, parsley, pine nuts and a drizzle of olive oil. Top with the bread tops.

bialy bread slabs

Onion is the key ingredient in these bread slabs. First, it's caramelized, then stirred right into the dough.

MAKES 4 bread slabs PREP TIME 15 minutes (plus resting) COOK TIME 22 minutes

3 tablespoons extra-virgin olive oil

½ onion, chopped

1 tablespoon poppy seeds

Salt

2 cups Silvana's All-Purpose Flour (page 15), plus more for dusting

1 (¼-ounce/7.5-g) package active dry yeast

1 teaspoon sugar

2 large egg whites, at room temperature, lightly beaten

¾ cup warm water

1. In a medium skillet, heat 1 tablespoon olive oil over medium-low heat. Add the onion and cook, stirring occasionally, until golden, about 12 minutes. Stir in the poppy seeds and a pinch of salt.

2. In a large bowl, whisk together the flour, yeast, 1 teaspoon salt and sugar. Add the egg whites, remaining 2 tablespoons olive oil, the onion mixture and water. Using a wooden spoon, beat until the dough pulls away from the sides of the bowl.

3. Turn the dough onto a lightly floured, 12-inch (30-cm)-long piece of parchment paper. Lightly flour the top and, using your fingertips or a rolling pin, press the dough out to form a rectangle about ¾ inch (1.5 cm) thick. Cover loosely with plastic wrap and let rest at room temperature for about 30 minutes. Cut into four equal pieces.

4. Position a rack in the bottom of the oven with a baking stone on the rack and preheat to 450°F. Brush each dough piece with olive oil and sprinkle with salt. Slide the dough pieces with parchment paper onto the preheated baking stone and bake until puffy and crisp on the bottom, about 10 minutes. Let cool on a wire rack.

french dip with caramelized onions and russian horseradish mayonnaise on bialy bread slabs

The juicy meat? The warm au jus? The soggy bread? What could be better?

SERVES 4 **PREP TIME** 15 minutes **COOK TIME** 30 minutes

1 tablespoon extra-virgin olive oil

1 medium onion, thinly sliced

1 teaspoon sugar

Salt and pepper

2 tablespoons balsamic vinegar

¼ cup mayonnaise

3 tablespoons ketchup

2 teaspoons prepared horseradish

½ teaspoon Worcestershire sauce

2 tablespoons plus 1 teaspoon finely chopped fresh flat-leaf parsley

2¼ cups chicken broth

2 tablespoons cornstarch

1 pound (500 g) deli-sliced roast beef

4 Bialy Bread Slabs (opposite page) or store-bought rolls, split and toasted

½ bunch watercress, stems trimmed

1. In a large skillet, heat the olive oil over medium-high heat. Add the onion, sugar and ¼ teaspoon salt and cook, stirring, until golden-brown, about 10 minutes. Add the vinegar, stirring to loosen any brown bits on the bottom of the skillet, and cook for about 1 minute.

2. Meanwhile, in a small bowl, whisk together the mayonnaise, ketchup, horseradish, Worcestershire sauce and 1 teaspoon parsley; refrigerate.

3. In a medium saucepan, heat 2 cups broth over high heat until reduced by a quarter, about 15 minutes. In a small bowl, mix together the remaining ¼ cup broth and cornstarch; whisk into the hot broth. Add the roast beef and remaining 2 table-spoons parsley and simmer on low heat until just warmed through, about 1 minute; season with about ½ teaspoon salt and ¼ teaspoon pepper.

4. To assemble, spread some horseradish mayonnaise on each bread bottom; top with some watercress, warm roast beef and caramelized onions. Spread more horseradish mayonnaise on each bread top and set into place. Cut in half diagonally and serve with the au jus for dipping.

perfect pizza crusts

There's no need to bloom the yeast or let the dough rise for hours before baking these pizza crusts. You can freeze the baked pizza crusts for up to 1 month. Just bring to room temperature before using. For the crispiest crust, use a baking stone, which you can order online for about $30.

MAKES Two 8½-inch (21-cm) pizza crusts (1 pound/500 g pizza dough)
PREP TIME 10 minutes (plus resting) BAKE TIME 16 minutes

2 cups Silvana's All-Purpose Flour (page 15), plus more for dusting

1 (¼-ounce/7.5-g) package active dry yeast

1 teaspoon sugar

1 teaspoon salt

2 large egg whites, at room temperature, lightly beaten

2 tablespoons extra-virgin olive oil, plus more for brushing

¾ cup warm water

1. In a large bowl, whisk together the flour, yeast, sugar and salt. Add the egg whites, olive oil and water. Using a wooden spoon, beat until the dough pulls away from the sides of the bowl.

2. Divide the dough into two equal pieces; place each on a lightly floured, 12-inch (30-cm)-long piece of parchment paper. Lightly flour the top and, using your fingertips or a rolling pin, press the dough out to make a round about ¼ inch (0.5 cm) thick. Cover loosely with plastic wrap and let rest at room temperature for about 30 minutes.

3. Position a rack in the bottom of the oven with a baking stone on the rack and preheat to 450°F. Working with one piece of dough at a time, slide the dough with parchment paper onto the preheated baking stone and bake until puffy and crisp on the bottom, about 8 minutes. Let cool on a wire rack. Repeat with the remaining dough.

VARIATION

cornmeal pizza crusts

Replace the water with ¾ cup rice milk, at room temperature, mixed with 1 teaspoon apple cider vinegar. Use 1¾ cups plus 2 tablespoons Silvana's All-Purpose Flour (page 15) mixed with ½ cup cornmeal (preferably medium grind) instead of the 2 cups flour above; mix and proceed as above.

1. Beat together the ingredients until the pizza dough forms.

2. Shape each piece of dough into a circle with a rolling pin.

3. Cover loosely with plastic wrap and let rest.

"This is the Isaiah standard—my 5-second tomato sauce with pepperoni. Dinner is served."

pepperoni pizza

Here's an example of how sometimes the simplest things can, in fact, be the most delicious. You can swap store-bought pizza sauce for the tomato sauce here.

MAKES 2 (8½-inch/21-cm) pizzas PREP TIME 5 minutes COOK TIME 16 minutes

1 cup tomato puree

½ tablespoon extra-virgin olive oil, plus more for brushing

¼ teaspoon salt

2 tablespoons water

2 (8½-inch/21-cm) baked Perfect Pizza Crusts (page 122) or store-bought baked pizza crusts

Crushed red pepper flakes, to taste

14 slices pepperoni (about 4 ounces/125 g), for topping

1. In a small bowl, stir together the tomato puree, olive oil, salt and water.

2. Position a rack in the bottom of the oven with a baking stone on the rack and preheat to 450°F. Working with one pizza crust at a time, brush with olive oil, sprinkle with red pepper flakes and spoon on about ¼ cup tomato mixture, leaving a ½-inch (1-cm) border of plain crust. Top with half of the pepperoni and bake until the crust is golden and the pepperoni is crisp, 6 to 8 minutes. Repeat with the remaining pizza crust and toppings.

chicken sausage, peppers and onions pizza

You can prepare the pizza sauce ahead of time and refrigerate it, covered, for up to 2 weeks.

MAKES 2 (8½-inch/21-cm) pizzas **PREP TIME** 15 minutes **COOK TIME** 36 minutes

2 tablespoons extra-virgin olive oil, plus more for brushing

1 teaspoon salt-packed capers—rinsed, drained and patted dry

1 teaspoon tomato paste

3 red bell peppers, 2 seeded and chopped, and 1 seeded and cut into ⅛-inch (.25-cm) rings

1 teaspoon balsamic vinegar

Salt

¼ cup water

2 (8½-inch/21-cm) baked Perfect Pizza Crusts (page 122) or store-bought baked pizza crusts

3 fully cooked sweet Italian chicken sausages (about 8 ounces/250 g), such as Applegate Farms, cut into ¼-inch (0.5-cm) cubes

½ red onion, cut into ⅛-inch (0.25-cm) rings

Fresh oregano, chopped, for topping

1. In a skillet, heat the olive oil over medium-high heat. Add the capers and cook until golden, about 1 minute. Stir in the tomato paste and cook for 1 minute. Stir in the chopped bell peppers and cook, stirring occasionally, until softened, about 8 minutes. Stir in the vinegar and cook until tender, about 10 minutes; season with about ¼ teaspoon salt. Transfer to a blender and add the water; puree until smooth.

2. Position a rack in the bottom of the oven with a baking stone on the rack and preheat to 450°F. Working with one pizza crust at a time, brush with olive oil. Spoon on about ¼ cup red pepper sauce, leaving a ½-inch (1-cm) border of plain crust. Top with half the sausage, bell pepper rings and onion rings. Bake until the crust is golden, 6 to 8 minutes; top with oregano. Repeat with the remaining pizza crust and toppings.

"There's no ordinary pizza sauce here. Instead of a tomato-based sauce, this one is made with red bell peppers and salty capers. The balsamic vinegar gives it a sweet yet acidic edge."

shrimp pizza with garlic cream sauce

Plain and simple, this is shrimp scampi on pizza. Flour is the secret behind the beautifully creamy sauce.

MAKES 2 (8½-inch/21-cm) pizzas **PREP TIME** 10 minutes **COOK TIME** 21 minutes

2 tablespoons extra-virgin olive oil, plus more for brushing

1 clove garlic, finely chopped

2 tablespoons Silvana's All-Purpose Flour (page 15)

¼ cup white wine

½ cup chicken broth

Salt and pepper

2 (8½-inch/21-cm) baked Perfect Pizza Crusts (page 122) or store-bought baked pizza crusts

8 ounces (250 g) rock shrimp (about 1 cup) or medium shrimp, peeled and deveined

Crushed red pepper flakes, for topping

Fresh parsley, finely chopped, for topping

1. In a large skillet, heat the olive oil over medium-high heat. Add the garlic and cook, stirring occasionally, until golden, about 1 minute. Sprinkle in the flour and stir for 1 minute. Stir in the wine and broth and simmer, stirring occasionally, until slightly thickened, about 3 minutes; season with 1 teaspoon salt and ½ teaspoon pepper.

2. Position a rack in the bottom of the oven with a baking stone on the rack and preheat to 450°F. Working with one pizza crust at a time, brush with olive oil. Spoon on about 3 table-spoons garlic cream sauce, leaving a ½-inch (1-cm) border of plain crust. Scatter over half of the shrimp and season with red pepper flakes. Bake until the crust is golden, 6 to 8 min-utes; top with parsley. Repeat with the remaining pizza crust and toppings.

From left to right: Barbecued Beef Pizza (page 130),
Shrimp Pizza with Garlic Cream Sauce (page 127) and
Chicken Sausage, Peppers and Onions Pizza (page 126)

barbecued beef pizza

If you're not into spicy, swap ketchup for the chili sauce in the spicy mayo sauce. It's fun to use a squeeze bottle, but if you don't have one on hand, just drizzle the sauce over the pizza with a fork.

MAKES 2 (8½-inch/21-cm) pizzas   PREP TIME 5 minutes   COOK TIME 20 minutes

½ cup Pineapple–Brown Sugar Barbecue Sauce (page 152)

½ cup tomato puree

Salt and pepper

½ pound (250 g) deli-sliced roast beef, torn into pieces

2 (8½-inch/21-cm) baked Perfect Pizza Crusts (page 122) or store-bought baked pizza crusts

Extra-virgin olive oil, for brushing

¼ cup mayonnaise

1½ teaspoons sriracha hot sauce, or to taste

1 tablespoon fresh lemon juice

2 teaspoons water

Radishes, thinly sliced, for topping

Fresh cilantro or parsley leaves, for topping

1. Position a rack in the bottom of the oven with a baking stone on the rack and preheat to 450°F. In a medium saucepan, combine the barbecue sauce and tomato puree and bring to a boil over medium-high heat; season with about ¼ teaspoon each salt and pepper. Add the roast beef and simmer until warmed through, about 1 minute.

2. Meanwhile, working with one pizza crust at a time, brush with olive oil. Using a slotted spoon, top with half of the barbecued beef, leaving a ½-inch (1-cm) border of plain crust. Bake until the crust is golden, 6 to 8 minutes.

3. While the pizza bakes, in a small bowl, combine the mayonnaise, hot sauce, lemon juice, water and about ⅛ teaspoon salt. Transfer to a squeeze bottle or a resealable plastic bag with the corner snipped off.

4. To serve, drizzle the spicy mayo sauce across the pizza. Scatter over radishes and cilantro. Repeat with the remaining pizza crust and toppings.

fried calamari pizza with garlic and hot pepper oil

You can adjust the heat in the garlic and hot pepper oil by adding more or less olive oil to the mix. Store the oil for up to 1 week at room temperature.

MAKES 2 (8½-inch/21-cm) pizzas PREP TIME 15 minutes COOK TIME 26 minutes

½ cup plus ½ tablespoon extra-virgin olive oil, plus more for brushing

2 cloves garlic, smashed and peeled

2 tablespoons crushed red pepper flakes, or to taste

Vegetable oil, for frying

1 cup Silvana's All-Purpose Flour (page 15)

8 ounces (250 g) cleaned squid, cut into ¼-inch (0.5-cm) rings

Salt

1 cup tomato puree

2 tablespoons water

2 (8½-inch/21-cm) baked Perfect Pizza Crusts (page 122) or store-bought baked pizza crusts

Celery, sliced, and celery leaves, chopped, for topping

1. To make the hot pepper oil, combine ¼ cup olive oil, the garlic and red pepper flakes in a blender and blend until combined, about 1 minute. With the motor running, stream in ¼ cup olive oil until smooth.

2. In a large pot, heat 2 inches (5 cm) of vegetable oil to 360°F. Place the flour in a large resealable plastic bag. Add the squid rings and toss to coat. Using a sieve and working over the sink, shake off the excess flour. Working in two batches, add the calamari to the hot oil and fry until golden, about 5 minutes. Transfer to paper towel–lined plates and sprinkle with salt.

3. Meanwhile, in a small bowl, combine the tomato puree, remaining ½ tablespoon olive oil, ¼ teaspoon salt and the water.

4. Position a rack in the bottom of the oven with a baking stone on the rack and preheat to 450°F. Working with one pizza crust at a time, brush with olive oil. Spoon on about ¼ cup tomato sauce, leaving a ½-inch (1-cm) border of plain crust. Top with half the fried calamari. Bake until the crust is golden, 6 to 8 minutes. Top with half the celery and celery leaves, and drizzle with the hot pepper oil. Repeat with the remaining pizza crust and toppings.

sandwiches & pizza

"This is an all-grilled pizza—from crust to toppings. I like to grill everything until slightly charred, which adds flavor and smokiness."

grilled vegetable pesto pizza

This pesto is light on the garlic, but if you like your garlic, go ahead and add more.

MAKES 2 (8½-inch/21-cm) pizzas **PREP TIME** 15 minutes **COOK TIME** 13 minutes

2 cups packed fresh basil leaves, plus more, chopped, for topping

½ cup walnuts

1 clove garlic, smashed

½ cup extra-virgin olive oil, plus more for brushing

Salt and pepper

½ small eggplant, sliced crosswise into ½-inch (1-cm) rounds

1 zucchini, sliced crosswise into ½-inch (1-cm) rounds

2 plum tomatoes, sliced crosswise into ½-inch (1-cm) rounds

4 ounces (125 g) asparagus, ends trimmed and cut into 3-inch (7.5-cm) pieces

1 pound (500 g) Perfect Pizza Crusts dough (page 122), or store-bought pizza dough, at room temperature and halved

1. To make the pesto, in a food processor, combine the basil, walnuts, garlic, olive oil and 1 teaspoon salt; process until smooth.

2. Preheat a grill or grill pan to medium-high heat. Brush the eggplant, zucchini, tomatoes and asparagus with olive oil; season generously with salt and pepper. Grill, turning once, until tender and slightly charred, about 5 minutes.

3. On a lightly oiled, inverted baking sheet, roll out 1 piece of pizza dough to make a round about ¼ inch (0.5 cm) thick; brush with olive oil. Repeat with the remaining dough. Shimmy each piece of pizza dough off the baking sheet and onto the grill and cook with the grill cover down (if you're using a grill pan, tent with aluminum foil) until the crust holds its shape and grill marks appear, about 3 minutes. Using a spatula, flip each crust over onto the coolest part of the grill. Spread about 3 tablespoons of the pesto over each pizza crust, leaving a ½-inch (1-cm) border of plain crust. Top each with half of the grilled vegetables. Cook with the grill cover down (or aluminum tent) until the crust is golden, 3 to 5 minutes. Remove the pizzas from the grill and top each with basil.

corn, jalapeño and bacon crumb cornmeal pizza

This pizza was inspired by the flavors of August. From the cornmeal crust to the corn topping, this pizza holds the season close, even as the cool fall breezes in.

MAKES 2 (8½-inch/21-cm) pizzas PREP TIME 10 minutes COOK TIME 20 minutes

1 cup rice cereal crumbs

4 slices bacon, cooked until crisp and crumbled

1½ tablespoons extra-virgin olive oil, plus more for brushing and drizzling

1½ tablespoons Silvana's All-Purpose Flour (page 15)

¾ cup chicken broth

Salt and pepper

2 (8½-inch/21-cm) baked Cornmeal Pizza Crusts (page 122)

2 cups corn kernels

2 jalapeños, seeded and thinly sliced into rings

Fresh cilantro or parsley, chopped, for topping

1. In a small bowl, stir together the cereal crumbs and bacon.

2. In a medium skillet, heat the olive oil over medium heat. Sprinkle in the flour and cook, stirring, for 1 minute. Gradually stir in the broth and simmer, stirring, until slightly thickened, about 3 minutes; season with about ½ teaspoon salt and ¼ teaspoon pepper.

3. Position a rack in the bottom of the oven with a baking stone on the rack and preheat to 450°F. Working with one pizza crust at a time, brush with olive oil. Spoon on about 3 table-spoons sauce, leaving a ½-inch (1-cm) border of plain crust. Top with half of the corn, half of the jalapeños and half of the bacon crumbs. Bake until the crust is golden, 6 to 8 minutes. Top with cilantro and drizzle with olive oil. Repeat with the remaining pizza crust and toppings.

"We're regulars at the farmers' market, where we find every fruit and vegetable you'd expect, including corn, the star ingredient in this pizza."

mini turkey meatball pizza

There are two things you should know about how to make a juicy meatball. First, when you shape the meat into balls, handle them as little as possible (no need for perfection here). Second, let the meatballs simmer in the tomato sauce until you're ready to top your pizza, to keep them nice and moist.

MAKES 2 (8½-inch/21-cm) pizzas PREP TIME 10 minutes COOK TIME 40 minutes

1 tablespoon extra-virgin olive oil, plus more for brushing and drizzling

1 (28-ounce/796-mL) can tomato puree

3 tablespoons finely chopped fresh basil, plus more for topping

Salt and pepper

8 ounces (250 g) ground turkey

1 medium red onion, ¼ cup finely chopped and ¼ cup thinly sliced

2 tablespoons rice cereal crumbs

1 large egg, lightly beaten

2 (8½-inch/21-cm) baked Perfect Pizza Crusts (page 122) or store-bought baked pizza crusts

1. In a large saucepan, heat the olive oil over medium heat. Stir in the tomato puree and bring to a boil. Stir in 2 tablespoons basil and season with about 1 teaspoon salt. Reduce the heat to low and let simmer.

2. Meanwhile, in a large bowl, combine the turkey, chopped onion, cereal crumbs, egg, remaining 1 tablespoon basil, ½ teaspoon salt and ¼ teaspoon pepper; shape into ½-inch (1-cm) balls. Add the meatballs to the tomato sauce, cover and simmer until cooked through, about 20 minutes.

3. Position a rack in the bottom of the oven with a baking stone on the rack and preheat to 450°F. Working with one pizza crust at a time, brush with olive oil. Using a slotted spoon, spoon on some of the meatballs and sauce, leaving a ½-inch (1-cm) border of plain crust. Top with half of the thinly sliced onion. Bake until the crust is golden, 6 to 8 minutes. Top with basil and drizzle with olive oil. Repeat with the remaining pizza crust and toppings.

main dishes

THERE WAS NEVER ANY DOUBT IN MY MIND that Isaiah was not going to be a vegetarian. When he was about 2 years old, we would sit in my mom's kitchen at his plastic Little Tikes picnic table and joke about having a steak-eating contest. He always won. Since then, I've worked hard to get him to like foods other than beef. It hasn't been easy, but now he'll eat shrimp and pork, and tolerate chicken if I cook it right. That said, anything with bacon makes it better. Or, if Isaiah can eat dinner with his fingers—chicken legs and shrimp fit nicely into this category—that works, too. His grandmothers have had perhaps the greatest influence on him, with their roast beef and oven-barbecued ribs, both tasty recipes that, for the most part, cook themselves in the oven and make great leftovers. I have more than embraced their contributions to our family table. My other tactic: Put my twist on tradition. So instead of chicken potpie, I'll make turkey potpie pockets. Before I know it, there's nothing left on Isaiah's plate.

"You can't replace what it feels like to sit down together at the table and enjoy good food and family."

"Isaiah and I love to eat breakfast for supper. We cozy up on the couch under a blanket with our occasional, much-needed

chicken and waffles with maple bacon gravy

This dish brings breakfast and supper together in a savory-sweet, comforting meal. You still get your waffles, and there's a whisper of warm maple syrup, too.

SERVES 4 PREP TIME 10 minutes COOK TIME 40 minutes

4 boneless chicken breasts (about 1½ pounds/750 g), with skin on

Extra-virgin olive oil

Salt and pepper

2 cups Silvana's Pancake Mix (page 15)

1 tablespoon plus ½ teaspoon dry mustard

1 teaspoon paprika

3 tablespoons finely chopped fresh parsley

2 large eggs, at room temperature,

¼ cup vegetable oil

3 cups rice milk

6 slices bacon, chopped

1 tablespoon pure maple syrup

1½ tablespoons cornstarch

½ teaspoon cayenne pepper

1. Preheat the oven to 425°F. Generously rub the chicken all over with olive oil; season generously with salt and pepper. Heat a large ovenproof skillet over high heat. Place the chicken skin side down in the hot skillet; cook until the skin is golden and crisp, about 4 minutes. Turn over and transfer the skillet to the oven; roast until cooked through, about 12 minutes. Let cool slightly; cut diagonally into slices.

2. Preheat a waffle iron to medium-high heat. In a large bowl, whisk together the pancake mix, 1 tablespoon dry mustard, paprika, 1 tablespoon parsley and ½ teaspoon salt.

3. In a small bowl, whisk together the eggs, vegetable oil and 1½ cups milk. Add to the pancake mix mixture and stir until just combined. Grease the waffle iron with nonstick cooking spray. Pour about ⅓ cup batter into each waffle iron square, spreading the batter out to the edges; close and cook until crisp, about 5 minutes. Repeat with the remaining batter.

4. Meanwhile, in the same skillet, cook the bacon over medium heat until crispy and the fat has rendered, about 3 minutes. Measure the rendered fat from the skillet and add enough olive oil to yield 3 tablespoons. Return to the skillet and add 1¼ cups milk and the maple syrup; bring to a boil, whisking occasionally, over medium-high heat.

5. In a small bowl, mix together the cornstarch, cayenne, remaining ½ teaspoon dry mustard and remaining ¼ cup milk; whisk into the maple mixture and boil until thickened, 8 to 10 minutes. Season with the remaining 2 tablespoons parsley, ¼ teaspoon salt and ⅛ teaspoon pepper. To serve, divide the waffles among four plates and top with the chicken and gravy.

main dishes

mashed potato–stuffed chicken

Add a vegetable and you're looking at a complete meal. In this recipe, you get chicken and potatoes in just one bite. Stuffing the chicken breasts keeps the meat tender and moist. Stir your favorite flavorings, like grated nutmeg or chopped chives, into the mashed potatoes.

SERVES 4 PREP TIME 30 minutes COOK TIME 1 hour 10 minutes

1 pound (500 g) Yukon gold potatoes (about 2 potatoes), peeled and cut into 1-inch (2.5-cm) pieces

¼ cup rice milk

5 tablespoons extra-virgin olive oil

Finely grated zest of ½ lemon, plus lemon wedges, for serving

Salt and pepper

4 bone-in chicken breasts (about 3½ pounds/2 kg)

2 tablespoons chopped fresh flat-leaf parsley

1. Preheat the oven to 400°F. In a medium saucepan, bring the potatoes and enough cold water to cover to a boil. Lower the heat and simmer until tender, about 20 minutes. Drain and return the potatoes to the saucepan. Add the milk, 4 table-spoons olive oil and lemon zest and mash until smooth; season with about ½ teaspoon salt and ⅛ teaspoon pepper.

2. Run your fingers under the skin of each chicken breast; stuff with one-quarter of the mashed potatoes, gently pressing to evenly distribute. Season the chicken with about ¾ teaspoon salt and ¼ teaspoon pepper. Place in a roasting pan; top with the parsley and drizzle with the remaining 1 tablespoon olive oil. Bake until golden and the juices run clear, about 50 minutes. Serve with lemon wedges.

"My husband, Stephen, first made these grilled potato slabs—thick-cut potato slices drizzled with olive oil, grilled and then generously salted."

grilled ketchup-glazed chicken with potato slabs

When you think of the ingredients in ketchup—tomatoes, sugar, vinegar—it makes sense to use it in a marinade. In this recipe, ketchup gives the chicken a shimmering, crunchy skin and deeply caramelized flavors.

SERVES 4 PREP TIME 5 minutes (plus marinating) COOK TIME 35 minutes

1 cup ketchup

2 tablespoons extra-virgin olive oil, plus more for drizzling

2 tablespoons apple cider vinegar

2 cloves garlic, smashed

¼ cup packed light brown sugar

2 teaspoons chili powder

Salt

8 chicken drumsticks (about 1½ pounds/750 g)

2 baking potatoes

Lime wedges, for serving

1. In a resealable plastic bag, combine the ketchup, olive oil, vinegar, garlic, brown sugar, chili powder and 1 teaspoon salt; reserve about ¼ cup for basting. Add the drumsticks, seal the bag and let marinate for about 30 minutes.

2. Meanwhile, preheat a grill or grill pan to high. Microwave the potatoes on high until slightly softened, 5 to 7 minutes. Slice the potatoes lengthwise about ¼ inch (0.5 cm) thick. Drizzle both sides with olive oil.

3. Grill the drumsticks, basting with the ketchup marinade and turning occasionally, until the skin is golden and crisp and the juices run clear, 25 to 30 minutes. In the last 10 minutes of cooking, grill the potatoes until grill marks appear, about 4 minutes on each side. Transfer to a plate and sprinkle generously with salt. Serve the chicken and potatoes with lime wedges.

main dishes

oven-fried frito chicken fingers with honey-mustard dip

You can swap tortilla chips for the Fritos and use store-bought salad dressing, barbecue sauce or just plain ketchup in place of the honey-mustard dip.

SERVES 6 PREP TIME 20 minutes COOK TIME 20 minutes

Extra-virgin olive oil, for greasing

6 cups corn chips, such as Fritos, coarsely crushed

Salt and pepper

3 large eggs, at room temperature

1½ pounds (750 g) chicken tenders

½ cup mayonnaise

2 tablespoons Dijon mustard

2 tablespoons honey

1 tablespoon fresh lemon juice

1. Preheat the oven to 425°F. Lightly grease a baking sheet with olive oil. In a shallow bowl, combine the corn chips, 1½ teaspoons salt and ½ teaspoon pepper. In another shallow bowl, beat the eggs. Coat a chicken tender with the corn chip mixture, dip into the eggs, then coat again with the corn chip mixture; place on the baking sheet. Repeat with the remaining chicken. Bake until golden and cooked through, about 20 minutes.

2. Meanwhile, in a small bowl, stir together the mayonnaise, mustard, honey and lemon juice; season with about ¼ teaspoon salt. Serve with the chicken fingers.

"What I like most about this predictably kid-friendly meal is that it's quick to make. Translation: I can get my kids fed fast and keep them happy, too."

roasted mushroom–stuffed chicken marsala

If you don't have marsala on hand, use white wine.

SERVES 4 **PREP TIME** 25 minutes **COOK TIME** 30 minutes

3 tablespoons extra-virgin olive oil

1 medium onion, finely chopped

1 pound (500 g) button mushrooms, thinly sliced

½ cup marsala or white wine

2 tablespoons chopped fresh parsley, plus more for topping

Salt and pepper

1 cup chicken broth

4 boneless chicken breasts, with skin on (about 2 pounds/ 1 kg), butterflied and pounded ½ inch (1 cm) thick

1. In a large skillet, heat 2 tablespoons olive oil over medium-high heat. Add the onion and cook until softened, about 3 minutes. Add the mushrooms and cook until softened, stirring occasionally, about 5 minutes. Stir in the marsala and parsley; bring to a simmer. Cook until reduced, about 2 minutes; season with about ¾ teaspoon salt and ¼ teaspoon pepper. Using a slotted spoon, transfer half of the mixture to a small bowl. To make the mushroom sauce, stir the broth into the skillet and cook to reduce slightly, about 3 minutes; cover and keep warm.

2. Preheat the oven to 350°F. Stuff each chicken breast with one-quarter of the mushroom mixture in the small bowl and tie with butcher's string to enclose; season the chicken with about ¾ teaspoon salt and ¼ teaspoon pepper.

3. In a large ovenproof skillet, heat the remaining 1 tablespoon olive oil over medium-high heat. Add the chicken skin side down and cook until golden and crisp, about 3 minutes. Turn skin side up and transfer to the oven; roast until cooked through, about 15 minutes. Top the chicken with the mushroom sauce and parsley.

rosemary-garlic roast chicken with root vegetables

This is a low-maintenance dinner that receives high praise from the family. If you're more of a chicken-and-potatoes person, just swap two russet or sweet potatoes for the parsnips.

SERVES 6 **PREP TIME** 15 minutes **COOK TIME** 1 hour 30 minutes

5 carrots, cut into ½-inch (1-cm) pieces

3 parsnips, peeled and cut into ½-inch (1-cm) pieces

2 onions, 1 cut into ½-inch (1-cm) pieces and 1 halved

4 cloves garlic, smashed

6 sprigs rosemary

¾ cup chicken broth

1 (5-pound/2.5-kg) roasting chicken, rinsed and patted dry

Salt and pepper

Extra-virgin olive oil, for brushing

1. Preheat the oven to 400°F. In a 10-inch by 14-inch (25-cm by 33-cm) baking pan, toss the carrots, parsnips, onion pieces, garlic and 3 sprigs rosemary with the broth; spread evenly in the pan.

2. Season the chicken cavity with salt and pepper. Stuff with the halved onion and remaining 3 sprigs rosemary and place breast side down in the middle of the pan. Brush the top of the chicken all over with olive oil and season with salt. Roast for 30 minutes. Turn the chicken breast side up and brush all over with olive oil; season generously with salt and pepper. Return the pan to the oven and continue to roast until the juices run clear, about 1 hour more. Cut the chicken into pieces and serve with the vegetables and any pan drippings.

turkey potpie pockets

While you're filling each potpie pocket, keep the remaining pieces of dough cold in the fridge.

SERVES 4 PREP TIME 30 minutes COOK TIME 30 minutes

1 tablespoon extra-virgin olive oil

2 tablespoons finely chopped onion

2 tablespoons finely chopped celery

2 tablespoons finely chopped carrot

½ cup sliced button mushrooms

1 tablespoon Silvana's All-Purpose Flour (page 15), plus more for dusting

½ teaspoon chopped fresh thyme leaves

¼ cup white wine

½ cup water

1 cup cooked turkey, cut into ½-inch (1-cm) pieces

2 teaspoons finely chopped fresh parsley

Salt and pepper

All-Purpose Pie Crust dough (page 213) or 2 pounds (1 kg) store-bought unsweetened pie crust dough, refrigerated

1 large egg beaten with 1 teaspoon water

1. Heat the olive oil in a large pot over medium-high heat. Add the onion, celery, carrot and mushrooms; cook until softened, about 5 minutes. Sprinkle the flour over the vegetables; stir for 30 seconds. Stir in the thyme, wine and water; bring to a boil and cook until slightly thickened, about 3 minutes. Stir in the turkey, parsley, ¼ teaspoon salt and ⅛ teaspoon pepper; let cool.

2. Meanwhile, divide the dough into four equal pieces. Turn each piece onto a lightly floured piece of parchment paper. Lightly flour the tops and roll out each piece of dough until about ¼ inch (0.5 cm) thick and 8 inches (24 cm) in diameter.

3. Position a rack in the bottom of the oven and preheat the oven to 400°F. Line a baking sheet with parchment paper. Mound ⅓ cup of the turkey mixture onto each dough piece, leaving a ½-inch (1-cm) border. Fold the dough over the filling; crimp the edges with a fork to seal. Brush with the egg mixture and cut a small vent in the top of each potpie pocket. Place on the prepared baking sheet about 1 inch (2.5 cm) apart. Bake until golden and crisp, about 30 minutes.

root beer–glazed roasted turkey with rosemary, cinnamon and cayenne

SERVES 8 to 10 PREP TIME 20 minutes COOK TIME 2 hours 30 minutes

2 cups root beer, such as Barq's or Stewart's

5½ cups chicken broth

1 tablespoon ground cinnamon

1 teaspoon cayenne pepper

6 tablespoons fresh rosemary leaves (about 20 sprigs)

Salt and pepper

1 (12-pound/6-kg) turkey, rinsed and patted dry

2 Granny Smith apples— peeled, cored and quartered

2 onions, peeled and quartered

Extra-virgin olive oil, for drizzling

1 cup water

¼ cup Silvana's All-Purpose Flour (page 15)

1. In a medium saucepan, combine the root beer and 2 cups broth; bring to a boil over medium-high heat. Decrease the heat to medium-low and simmer until reduced to about ½ cup, about 1 hour and 15 minutes.

2. In a small bowl, stir together the cinnamon, cayenne, 2 tablespoons rosemary, 2 teaspoons salt and 1 teaspoon pepper.

3. Place a rack in the lower part of the oven and preheat to 450°F. Using your fingers, loosen the skin from the turkey breast and evenly spread the remaining 4 tablespoons rosemary. Season the turkey cavity with salt and pepper; place half of the apples and half of the onions inside. Place the turkey breast side up on a rack in a roasting pan; tuck in the wings and loosely tie together the drumsticks. Rub with the spice mixture; drizzle generously with olive oil. Place the remaining apples and onions around the turkey; pour ½ cup broth and ½ cup water into the pan.

4. Place the turkey in the oven, reduce the temperature to 350°F and roast for 1 hour. Remove the turkey from the oven and brush with some of the root beer glaze. Add ½ cup broth and the remaining ½ cup water to the pan; cover loosely with foil. Continue to roast, brushing occasionally with the glaze, until an instant-read thermometer inserted in the thigh without touching the bone registers 165°F, about 1 hour. Transfer the turkey to a platter, cover loosely with foil and let rest for at least 30 minutes before carving.

5. Meanwhile, strain the pan drippings into a 4-cup measuring cup; skim off any fat. Add enough broth to measure 4 cups and return to the pan. Place the roasting pan over two burners and bring to a boil over medium-high heat, scraping up any browned bits; simmer until slightly reduced, about 5 minutes. Sprinkle the flour on top; stir for 1 minute. Continue to simmer, stirring occasionally, until slightly thickened, about 5 minutes; season with salt and pepper. Serve the gravy with the turkey.

main dishes

Clockwise from upper left: Double-Crusted Double Apple Pie (page 212), German Chocolate Pecan Pie Bars (page 197), Bacon-Apple Cornbread Stuffing (page 176), Root Beer–Glazed Roasted Turkey with Rosemary, Cinnamon and Cayenne (page 147), Marshmallow-Topped Yam-and-Chipotle Bake (page 179) and Arugula Salad with Bacon-Walnut Praline, Pomegranate and Apple Cider Vinaigrette (page 77)

grilled sweet-and-sour apple slaw–topped burgers

This recipe makes extra slaw, enough to serve on the side.

SERVES 4 **PREP TIME** 25 minutes **COOK TIME** 12 minutes

slaw

1 tablespoon fresh lemon juice

1 tablespoon apple cider vinegar

1 teaspoon whole-grain mustard

1 teaspoon poppy seeds

1 teaspoon pure maple syrup

Salt and pepper

¼ cup extra-virgin olive oil

3 cups shredded green cabbage

1 celery stalk, finely chopped (about ¼ cup)

2 apples

maple mayonnaise

½ cup mayonnaise

1 tablespoon whole-grain mustard

1 teaspoon pure maple syrup

1 tablespoon fresh lemon juice

burgers

1½ pounds (750 g) ground pork

2 tablespoons Pineapple–Brown Sugar Barbecue Sauce (page 152) or store-bought barbecue sauce

1 tablespoon pure maple syrup

Salt and pepper

4 baked Bread Slabs (page 116) or store-bought rolls, split and toasted

1. To make the slaw, in a large bowl, whisk together the lemon juice, vinegar, mustard, poppy seeds, maple syrup, 1¼ teaspoons salt and ½ teaspoon pepper. Whisk in the olive oil in a slow, steady stream. Add the cabbage and celery; toss. Peel and core the apples, then shred and toss with the cabbage mixture.

2. To make the maple mayonnaise, in a small bowl, combine the mayonnaise, mustard, maple syrup and lemon juice.

3. Preheat a grill or grill pan to medium heat. To make the burgers, in a large bowl, combine the pork, barbecue sauce, maple syrup, ¾ teaspoon salt and ¼ teaspoon pepper. Shape into four 1-inch (2.5-cm)-thick burgers. Grill, turning once, until cooked through and slightly charred, 8 to 10 minutes.

4. To assemble, spread the maple mayonnaise on the bread bottoms. Top each with a burger, slaw and a bread top.

"I've been to New Orleans only once, but my experiences and the spicy, complex flavors of its cuisine will play with my senses for a lifetime."

jambalaya-stuffed peppers with scallion crumbs

You can stuff the peppers up to 1 day ahead of time and keep them refrigerated until you're ready to cook.

SERVES 4 **PREP TIME** 25 minutes **COOK TIME** 40 minutes

½ cup plus 2 tablespoons extra-virgin olive oil, plus more for drizzling

5 large bell peppers, 4 caps removed and reserved, seeds and white membranes discarded, and 1 bell pepper, chopped

1 small onion, chopped

2 stalks celery, chopped

2 cloves garlic, finely chopped

8 ounces (227 g) shrimp— peeled, deveined and chopped

2 andouille sausages (about 8 ounces/250 g), halved lengthwise and cut into ¼-inch (0.5-cm) pieces

¾ teaspoon cayenne pepper

Salt and pepper

¾ cup rice cereal crumbs

3 tablespoons finely chopped scallion greens

2 medium tomatoes, chopped

½ cup Arborio rice

1. Preheat the oven to 400°F. In a medium skillet, heat 2 tablespoons olive oil over medium-high heat. Add the chopped bell pepper, onion, celery and garlic; cook until softened, about 5 minutes. Stir in the shrimp and sausage; cook until browned, about 3 minutes. Season with ½ teaspoon cayenne, 1 teaspoon salt and ¼ teaspoon pepper.

2. Meanwhile, in a small bowl, combine the cereal crumbs with the scallions, remaining ¼ teaspoon cayenne and ¼ teaspoon salt.

3. In a large bowl, stir together the tomatoes, rice, remaining ½ cup olive oil and bell pepper mixture; season with ½ teaspoon salt and ¼ teaspoon pepper.

4. Stand the whole bell peppers upright in a baking dish. Stuff each pepper with one-quarter of the jambalaya; bake, uncovered, for 35 minutes. Remove from the oven; top with the crumb mixture and drizzle with olive oil. Return to the oven and bake until the rice is cooked through, about 15 minutes more.

main dishes

Penny's sticky pineapple–brown sugar barbecued ribs

If you want to remove the thin membrane on the backside of the ribs, loosen a corner with a sharp knife, grip tightly and tear it off. Or ask your butcher to do you the favor.

SERVES 4   PREP TIME 5 minutes (plus marinating)   COOK TIME 2 hours 25 minutes

2 racks pork spareribs
(about 4 pounds/2 kg)

Salt and pepper

4 cups Pineapple–
Brown Sugar Barbecue
Sauce (see below)

1. Season the ribs all over with salt and pepper. Place the ribs and about 3 cups barbecue sauce in a jumbo resealable plastic bag; cover and refrigerate for at least 1 hour and up to overnight.

2. Preheat the oven to 300°F. Line two rimmed baking sheets with aluminum foil. Place the ribs on the prepared baking sheets, meaty side up. Roast, basting occasionally with the remaining 1 cup barbecue sauce, until tender, about 2 hours. Let cool for about 5 minutes. Cut into individual ribs.

pineapple–brown sugar barbecue sauce

This barbecue sauce will keep in the refrigerator for up to 2 weeks or in the freezer for 1 month. For super-saucy ribs, brush on warmed barbecue sauce just before serving.

MAKES 4 cups   PREP TIME 5 (plus cooling)   COOKING TIME 20 minutes

1 (8-ounce/216-mL) can
crushed pineapple in juice

2 cups ketchup

¼ cup Worcestershire sauce

¼ cup Louisiana-style hot
sauce, such as Frank's
RedHot, or to taste

¼ cup apple cider vinegar

2 tablespoons honey

2 teaspoons Dijon mustard

¼ cup water

½ cup packed light
brown sugar

1 teaspoon ground ginger

Salt and pepper

In a medium pot, combine the pineapple with its juice, ketchup, Worcestershire sauce, hot sauce, vinegar, honey, mustard, water, brown sugar and ginger; bring to a boil over medium-high heat. Reduce the heat to medium-low and simmer, stirring occasionally, until thickened, about 15 minutes. Season with salt and pepper. Let cool.

"My mom is famous—yes, famous—for her ribs. Sure, this is partly due to her low-and-slow cooking technique, but mostly it comes down to her barbecue sauce."

maple-mustard pork loin with roasted potatoes

This quick maple mustard is both sweet and pungent, with just a little heat that will wake you up ever so gently at first bite. Any leftover pork makes a great sandwich slathered with mayonnaise.

SERVES 6 PREP TIME 25 minutes (plus marinating and resting) COOK TIME 1 hour 10 minutes

¼ cup Dijon mustard

2 tablespoons pure maple syrup

¾ teaspoon hot sauce, such as Tabasco, or to taste

2 teaspoons chopped fresh rosemary, plus 6 sprigs

4 cloves garlic, smashed and peeled

4 tablespoons extra-virgin olive oil

1 (4-pound/2-kg) boneless pork loin

12 slices bacon

6 small baking potatoes (about 1½ pounds/ 750 g), quartered

Salt and pepper

1. In a large resealable plastic bag, combine the mustard, maple syrup, hot sauce, chopped rosemary, garlic and 2 tablespoons olive oil. Add the pork and turn to coat; refrigerate for at least 1 hour or overnight.

2. Preheat the oven to 375°F. Place the rosemary sprigs in the center of a roasting pan. Arrange six 14-inch (5-cm) lengths of kitchen string crosswise, about 2 inches (5 cm) apart, in the pan. Place the marinated pork on top of the strings and rosemary. Lay the bacon slices on an angle over the pork loin. Tie each string around the meat to secure the bacon; trim the loose ends.

3. Scatter the potatoes around the pork and drizzle with the remaining 2 tablespoons olive oil; toss. Season the pork and potatoes with ½ teaspoon salt and ¼ teaspoon pepper. Roast, stirring the potatoes occasionally, until an instant-read thermometer inserted into the center of the pork registers 150°F, about 1 hour. Let rest for 10 minutes before slicing.

"This is one of my weekend dishes that simmers in the background of our lives while we busy away the day."

pork and beans with butternut squash ragù

Just as you'd expect, the pork melts in your mouth, a result that only comes with a calm, lingering braise in the oven. You'll want to soak up the ragù with bread slabs or even stuff it between savory waffles—a messy but gratifying option.

SERVES 6 PREP TIME 20 minutes COOK TIME 2 hours 20 minutes

2 tablespoons extra-virgin olive oil

2 pounds (1 kg) boneless pork shoulder, trimmed, cut into 1-inch (2.5-cm) pieces and patted dry

1 medium onion, chopped

1 carrot, chopped

2 cloves garlic, smashed

2 rosemary sprigs

2 oregano sprigs

1 bay leaf

2 (10-ounce/300-g) bags frozen butternut squash pieces (about 3 cups)

1 teaspoon smoked or sweet paprika

1 teaspoon cayenne, or to taste

1 cup white wine or water

2 cups chicken broth

Salt and pepper

1 (15.5-ounce/540-mL) can cannellini beans, rinsed and drained

1. Preheat the oven to 325°F. In a large Dutch oven, heat the olive oil over medium-high heat. Working in batches, add the pork and cook, turning once, until browned, about 5 minutes; transfer to a plate. Add the onion, carrot, garlic, rosemary, oregano and bay leaf; cook over medium heat until softened, about 5 minutes. Add the squash, paprika and cayenne. Stir in the wine and simmer until slightly reduced, about 3 minutes. Return the pork to the pan and add the broth; bring to a boil. Season with ¾ teaspoon salt and ½ teaspoon pepper. Cover with a lid and transfer to the oven.

2. Cook until the pork is tender, about 1 hour and 45 minutes. Stir in the beans and cook, uncovered, until warmed through, about 15 minutes more. Before serving, remove the rosemary, oregano and bay leaf.

main dishes

roasted red pepper–crusted salsa meatloaf pie with tortilla chip crumbs

No need to make a pie crust for this recipe. Instead, line the pie plate with roasted red peppers, which will get you more flavor with less mess.

SERVES 6 **PREP TIME** 15 minutes (plus cooling) **COOK TIME** 45 minutes

Extra-virgin olive oil, for greasing and drizzling

1 (12-ounce/280-mL) jar roasted red peppers—drained, split, seeded and patted dry

1½ cups finely crushed tortilla chips

6 tablespoons chopped fresh flat-leaf parsley, plus more for topping

Salt and pepper

1½ pounds (750 g) ground beef

2 large eggs, lightly beaten

1 (16-ounce/430-mL) jar salsa

1. Preheat the oven to 375°F. Grease a 9-inch (22.5-cm) pie plate with olive oil and line with the red peppers. In a small bowl, mix together ½ cup crushed tortilla chips and 2 tablespoons parsley; season with ¼ teaspoon salt and ⅛ teaspoon pepper.

2. In a large bowl, mix the beef, eggs, ¾ cup salsa, the remaining 1 cup crushed tortilla chips, the remaining 4 tablespoons parsley, 1 teaspoon salt and 1 teaspoon pepper until just combined. Press the meat mixture into the pepper-lined pie plate. Spread the remaining salsa over the top, sprinkle with the tortilla chip mixture and drizzle with olive oil; bake for 45 minutes. Let cool for about 15 minutes, then top with parsley and cut into wedges.

"My mother-in-law, Marcia, cooks a mean roast. I can only hope that mine comes in a close second."

roast beef with horseradish sauce

In this recipe the meat is cooked to medium-rare; for medium, cook the roast until it registers 160°F on an instant-read thermometer.

SERVES 8 **PREP TIME** 15 minutes (plus resting) **COOK TIME** 1 hour

2 teaspoons finely chopped fresh thyme leaves

2 teaspoons finely chopped garlic

1 tablespoon finely grated orange zest (from about 1 orange)

1 tablespoon chili powder

1 tablespoon sesame seeds, toasted

Salt and pepper

2 tablespoons extra-virgin olive oil, plus more for rubbing

1 (4-pound/2-kg) beef eye of round roast, patted dry and tied with butcher's string

½ cup mayonnaise

1 (6-ounce/175-g) jar prepared horseradish, drained

2 teaspoons Dijon mustard

1 teaspoon apple cider vinegar

1 tablespoon sugar

1. Preheat the oven to 350°F. In a small bowl, combine the thyme, garlic, orange zest, chili powder, sesame seeds, 1 tablespoon salt and 2 teaspoons pepper. Rub the roast all over with olive oil, then pat all over with the spice blend.

2. In a roasting pan, heat the olive oil over medium-high heat. Add the roast and cook, turning, until browned, about 5 minutes. Transfer to the oven and roast until medium-rare, 45 to 50 minutes, or until an instant-read thermometer inserted into the thickest part of the meat registers 145°F. Transfer the roast to a cutting board and let rest for 20 minutes.

3. Meanwhile, in a small bowl, combine the mayonnaise, horseradish, mustard, vinegar and sugar until blended. Season with about ½ teaspoon salt and ⅛ teaspoon pepper.

4. Slice the roast about ¼ inch (0.5 cm) thick. Serve with the horseradish sauce.

grilled BBQ onion–smothered double bacon burgers

The recipe title says it all. But the real hero here is not the bacon, the barbecued onions or even the juicy burger itself—it's the Bialy Bread Slab. A good burger is nothing without the right bun.

SERVES 4 **PREP TIME** 10 minutes **COOK TIME** 30 minutes

12 slices bacon

2 sweet onions, such as Vidalias, cut crosswise into ¼-inch (0.5-cm) slices

½ cup Pineapple–Brown Sugar Barbecue Sauce (page 152) or store-bought barbecue sauce

Salt and pepper

1½ pounds (750 g) ground beef chuck

1 tablespoon Worcestershire sauce

Mayonnaise, for serving

4 Bialy Bread Slabs (page 120) or store-bought rolls, split and grilled

Shredded iceberg lettuce, for topping

1. Preheat a grill or grill pan to medium. In a large skillet, cook the bacon, turning once, until crisp, about 10 minutes; drain on paper towels. Crumble four slices.

2. Brush the onions with the barbecue sauce; season with salt and pepper. Grill, turning once and basting occasionally, until softened, about 10 minutes.

3. Meanwhile, in a medium bowl, combine the beef, crumbled bacon, Worcestershire sauce, 1 teaspoon salt and ½ teaspoon pepper. Shape into four 1-inch (2.5-cm)-thick burgers. Place the burgers on the grill, cover and cook, turning once, until cooked through and slightly charred, about 8 minutes for medium-rare.

4. Spread mayonnaise on each bread bottom. Top each with shredded lettuce, 1 burger, 2 slices bacon, some barbecued onions and the bread tops.

"Slowly my taco dinners evolved from ground beef to skirt steak. I like to make a Coca-Cola marinade, but you could also use Dr Pepper. If you're not into soda, just leave it out."

grilled spiced skirt steak tacos

The advantage to using steak in tacos is that once you throw the meat on the grill or under the broiler, it's ready in less than 10 minutes.

SERVES 4 PREP TIME 15 minutes (plus marinating) COOK TIME 8 minutes

1 small onion, chopped

Juice of 2 limes, plus lime wedges for serving

2 tablespoons extra-virgin olive oil

½ cup cola, such as Coca-Cola

4 tablespoons finely chopped fresh cilantro or parsley

2 teaspoons chili powder

¼ teaspoon ground cumin

Salt

1 (1-pound/500-g) skirt steak, cut into 4 equal pieces

2 medium tomatoes (about ¾ pound/375 g), finely chopped

2 jalapeños, seeded and finely chopped

8 crisp corn taco shells

2 cups shredded lettuce

1 avocado, chopped, for serving

1. In a resealable plastic bag, combine half the onion, half the lime juice, olive oil, cola, 2 tablespoons cilantro, chili powder, cumin and 1½ teaspoons salt. Add the steak; marinate at room temperature for about 30 minutes, or refrigerate overnight.

2. To make the salsa, in a medium bowl, toss together the tomatoes, remaining onion, remaining lime juice, remaining 2 tablespoons cilantro and jalapeños; season with about ¾ teaspoon salt.

3. Preheat a grill or grill pan to high. Grill the steak, turning once, until medium-rare, about 8 minutes. Let the steak rest for 5 minutes, then thinly slice against the grain into ¼-inch (0.5-cm)-thick slices. Toss with the salsa.

4. To assemble, fill each taco shell with some lettuce, avocado and steak strips with salsa. Serve with lime wedges.

spinach-stuffed braciola with tomato gravy

The braciola is delicious when it comes out of the oven, but it's even tastier the next day plated over salads or chopped up in a frittata.

SERVES 6 PREP TIME 30 minutes COOK TIME 1 hour 30 minutes

½ cup rice cereal crumbs

3 cloves garlic, 2 smashed and 1 finely chopped

2 tablespoons chopped flat-leaf parsley, plus more for serving

1 tablespoon extra-virgin olive oil, plus more for rubbing

1 (2-pound/1-kg) flank steak, pounded into a ½-inch (1-cm)-thick rectangle

Salt and pepper

8 slices ham

1 (10-ounce/300-g) package frozen spinach, thawed and squeezed dry

6 slices bacon, chopped

1 small onion, chopped

1 cup dry white wine or water

1 (28-ounce/796-mL) can chopped tomatoes with juice

1 teaspoon crushed red pepper flakes, or to taste

1. In a medium bowl, combine the cereal crumbs, chopped garlic, parsley and olive oil.

2. On a clean work surface, rub the steak with olive oil; generously season with about ¾ teaspoon salt and ¼ teaspoon pepper. Top with the ham and spinach, leaving a ½-inch (1-cm) border. Evenly spread the crumb mixture on top and roll, jelly-roll style; tie in several places.

3. In a large pan, cook the bacon over medium heat until the fat has rendered, about 3 minutes. Add the smashed garlic and the onion; cook until softened, about 3 minutes. Using a slotted spoon, transfer the bacon and onions to a bowl. Add the meat to the pan and cook, turning, until browned all over, about 10 minutes. Add the wine and cook until reduced by half, about 5 minutes. Stir in the tomatoes, red pepper flakes and bacon mixture. Reduce the heat, cover and simmer until cooked through, about 1 hour. Season with about ¼ teaspoon each salt and pepper. Transfer the meat to a platter; let stand for about 15 minutes. To serve, thinly slice the braciola diagonally and top with tomato gravy and parsley.

main dishes

sweet chile salmon with jalapeño slaw

The light crumb coating on the salmon adds a crunch and keeps the salmon juicy and tender.

SERVES 4 **PREP TIME** 15 minutes **COOK TIME** 12 minutes

Finely grated zest of 1 lime plus 3 tablespoons lime juice

¼ cup plus 1½ tablespoons store-bought Thai sweet red chili sauce, such as Thai Kitchen

2 tablespoons chopped fresh cilantro or parsley

¼ cup extra-virgin olive oil, plus more for greasing and drizzling

Salt

1 seedless cucumber, peeled and cut into matchsticks

½ red onion, cut into matchsticks

1 red bell pepper, seeded and cut into matchsticks

2 jalapeño peppers, seeded and cut into matchsticks

Four 1-inch (2.5-cm)-thick center-cut salmon fillets (6 ounces/175 g each), with skin on

½ cup rice cereal crumbs

1. To make the slaw, in a medium bowl, whisk together the lime zest, 2 tablespoons lime juice, 1½ tablespoons chili sauce and cilantro. In a slow, steady stream, whisk in the olive oil until blended; season with about ¼ teaspoon salt. Add the cucumber, onion, bell pepper and jalapeños to the dressing; toss to coat. Cover and refrigerate.

2. Preheat the oven to 425°F and lightly grease a baking sheet with olive oil. In a small bowl, stir together the remaining ¼ cup chili sauce and remaining 1 tablespoon lime juice.

3. Place the salmon skin side down on the prepared baking sheet; season generously with salt. Brush with the chili-lime sauce. Sprinkle over the crumbs and drizzle generously with olive oil; roast until cooked through, about 12 minutes. To serve, divide the fish among four plates and top with the slaw.

"This is one of my most highly complimented main-dish recipes. It also happens to be one of my easiest."

scampi-stuffed roasted shrimp

If there's no turmeric in your pantry, no worries—just leave it out.

SERVES 4   PREP TIME 35 minutes   COOK TIME 20 minutes

1 pound (500 g) medium shrimp—shelled, deveined and finely chopped

2 cloves garlic, finely chopped

¼ cup mayonnaise

1 cup rice cereal crumbs

2 tablespoons white wine

¼ teaspoon turmeric

¼ teaspoon crushed red pepper flakes

2 tablespoons finely chopped fresh parsley

Salt and pepper

16 jumbo shrimp (about 1½ pounds/750 g)— shelled, deveined and butterflied

Extra-virgin olive oil, for brushing

Lemon wedges, for serving

1. Preheat the oven to 425°F. Lightly grease a baking sheet. In a large bowl, mix together the chopped shrimp, garlic, mayonnaise, cereal crumbs, white wine, turmeric, red pepper flakes, parsley, ½ teaspoon salt and ¼ teaspoon pepper.

2. Place the jumbo shrimp butterflied side down on the prepared baking sheet. Mound about 2 tablespoons shrimp stuffing onto each shrimp, pressing gently; brush generously with olive oil and bake until golden, about 20 minutes. Serve with lemon wedges.

grilled shrimp with chickpea-rosemary relish

The trick with shrimp is to not overcook them. Grill until the shrimp just turn opaque, so they're tender, not tough.

SERVES 4 **PREP TIME** 15 minutes **COOK TIME** 5 minutes

1 tablespoon finely chopped rosemary

½ small red onion, finely chopped

1 tablespoon white wine vinegar

Finely grated zest and juice of 1 lemon

¼ cup extra-virgin olive oil, plus more for brushing

¼ teaspoon crushed red pepper flakes, or to taste

Salt

2 (15.5-ounce/540-mL) cans chickpeas, rinsed and drained

20 jumbo shrimp (about 2 pounds/1 kg), peeled and deveined, with tails intact

1. To make the relish, in a medium bowl, stir together the rosemary, onion, vinegar, lemon zest and lemon juice. In a slow, steady stream, whisk in the olive oil until blended; season with the red pepper flakes and about ½ teaspoon salt. Stir in the chickpeas.

2. Preheat a grill or grill pan to medium-high. Brush the shrimp with olive oil and season with about ¼ teaspoon salt. Thread five shrimp on each of four skewers. Place on the grill, cover, and grill, turning once, until firm and charred, about 5 minutes total. To serve, spoon the relish onto each of four plates and top with the shrimp.

fried sole with creamy lemon-pickle relish

You can substitute turbot or flounder for the sole.

SERVES 4 **PREP TIME** 20 minutes **COOK TIME** 25 minutes

Finely grated zest and
juice of 1 lemon

2 tablespoons mayonnaise

¼ cup extra-virgin olive oil

4 sweet gherkins,
finely chopped

1 teaspoon finely chopped
chives

Salt and pepper

¼ cup cornmeal

½ cup Silvana's
All-Purpose Flour (page 15)

1 teaspoon chili powder

2 large egg yolks

1 cup cold seltzer

½ cup vegetable oil, for frying

8 sole fillets
(about 1½ pounds/750 g)

1. To make the relish, in a medium bowl, whisk together the lemon zest, lemon juice and mayonnaise. In a slow, steady stream, whisk in the olive oil until blended. Stir in the gherkins and chives; season with about ¼ teaspoon salt and ⅛ teaspoon pepper.

2. In a medium bowl, whisk together the cornmeal, flour, chili powder, ½ teaspoon salt and ¼ teaspoon pepper. Add the egg yolks and seltzer; whisk until just combined.

3. In a large nonstick skillet, heat ¼ cup vegetable oil over medium-high heat until shimmering, about 3 minutes. Working in batches, dip the fish into the batter and add to the oil; cook, turning once, until golden, 4 to 6 minutes total. Drain on paper towels and sprinkle with salt. Halfway through cooking, clean out the pan and add another ¼ cup oil. Serve the fish with the relish.

main dishes

black bean, corn and yellow rice enchiladas with guacamole and red chile sauce

You can add roasted chicken or eggplant to the bean mixture. If you're short on time, swap in store-bought enchilada sauce or salsa verde for the red chile sauce.

SERVES 8 **PREP TIME** 20 minutes **COOK TIME** 50 minutes

2 tablespoons extra-virgin olive oil, plus more for greasing and brushing

1 large onion, finely chopped

3 cloves garlic, 1 smashed and 2 finely chopped

2 tablespoons ancho chile powder

2 cups dry red wine

1 (28-ounce/796-mL) can tomato puree

2 tablespoons honey

3 cups water

Salt

1 cup long-grain white rice

1 teaspoon ground cumin

2 teaspoons ground turmeric

8 corn tortillas

1 (15.5-ounce/540-mL) can black beans, rinsed and drained

1 cup corn kernels

2 ripe Hass avocados

Juice of 1 lime (about 2 tablespoons)

4 tablespoons chopped fresh cilantro or parsley

1. In a large saucepan, heat the olive oil over medium-high heat. Add the onion and finely chopped garlic and cook until softened, about 5 minutes. Add the chile powder and toast for 1 minute. Add the wine and bring to a boil; simmer until reduced, about 5 minutes. Add the tomato puree, honey and 1 cup water; cook for 15 minutes. Season with about 2 teaspoons salt.

2. In a medium saucepan with a tight-fitting lid, combine the smashed garlic, rice, cumin, turmeric, 1½ teaspoons salt and remaining 2 cups water; bring to a boil over medium-high heat. Cover, reduce the heat to low and simmer until the water is absorbed, about 15 minutes. Let sit, covered, for 5 minutes; fluff with a fork.

3. Preheat the oven to 450°F. Grease a large baking dish. Place 1 cup chile sauce in a shallow bowl and, working one at a time, dip the tortillas in the sauce and place on a plate. Spoon 2 heaping tablespoons rice, 1 heaping tablespoon beans and 1 heaping tablespoon corn down the center of the tortilla; roll up to enclose and place seam side down in the prepared baking dish. Repeat with the remaining tortillas, rice, beans and corn. Brush the enchiladas with olive oil and bake, uncovered, until golden around the edges, about 5 minutes.

4. Meanwhile, to make the guacamole, mash together the avocados, lime juice, ½ teaspoon salt and 2 tablespoons cilantro.

5. To assemble, pour the remaining sauce down the middle of the enchiladas and top with the remaining 2 tablespoons cilantro; serve with the guacamole.

vegetables & sides

I AM NOT THE BEST ROLE MODEL FOR MY KIDS when it comes to eating vegetables. I have had to teach not only them but also myself how delicious vegetables can taste. Maybe I have an aversion to vegetables because whenever I visited my nana Bernice in Miami Beach, she overcooked everything. Vegetables were no exception. As my mother used to say about Nana, if the Green Giant didn't freeze it, then we didn't eat it—and overcooking food was the norm back then. Does anyone like watery green beans or mushy peas? I've made a real effort to make simple, flavorful recipes that keep the integrity of the vegetable intact. Translation: Vegetables can be, and will be, crisp and bright green. One of Isaiah's earliest loves was asparagus, and Chiara will eat up sugar snap peas anywhere, anytime. And me? I'm taking it all in.

"For years, Isaiah wouldn't eat anything green. Not broccoli. Not spinach (raw or cooked). Not even a speck of parsley. It's still not easy, but I keep trying."

oven-fried french fries

For extra-golden, extra-crispy fries, follow these simple rules: Rinse the surface starch off the potatoes and, just as you'd heat a pan before cooking, preheat the baking sheet before oven-frying. Russet potatoes make for a fluffy, not mealy, French fry. You will see and taste the difference. If you want to fancy up your fries, toss in chopped parsley or rosemary, or swap chili powder for the paprika.

SERVES 4 **PREP TIME** 5 minutes **COOK TIME** 35 minutes

3 large russet potatoes (about 2 pounds/1 kg), cut lengthwise into ¼-inch (0.5-cm) sticks

2 tablespoons extra-virgin olive oil

Salt

1 teaspoon paprika

Ketchup, for serving

1. Fill a large bowl with water and add the cut potatoes; drain and dry well.

2. Preheat the oven to 425°F; heat a baking sheet for at least 5 minutes. In a large bowl, toss the potatoes with the olive oil; place on the preheated baking sheet, spreading out in a single layer, and season with about 1 teaspoon salt. Bake, turning occasionally, until golden and crisp, about 35 minutes. Season with the paprika and more salt, if desired. Serve with ketchup.

vegetables & sides

creamed olive oil–mashed potatoes

Once you taste these mashed potatoes, undoubtedly they'll become your family's most requested side dish. You get creaminess from Yukon gold potatoes and buttery nuttiness from the walnut oil. If you don't have walnut oil, just add more olive oil. For the softest, smoothest consistency, use a potato ricer, or run the potatoes through a food mill or sieve.

SERVES 4 **PREP TIME** 5 minutes **COOK TIME** 15 minutes

3 large Yukon gold potatoes (about 2 pounds/1 kg), peeled and cut into 1-inch (2.5-cm) pieces

1 cup rice milk

2 tablespoons extra-virgin olive oil

1 tablespoon walnut oil

Salt and pepper

1. In a large pot of salted water, bring the potatoes to a boil. Reduce the heat to medium and cook until tender, about 10 minutes; drain and reserve the pot.

2. Meanwhile, in a small saucepan, heat the milk over medium heat until warm, about 4 minutes; cover and keep warm.

3. Using a potato ricer and working in batches, press the potatoes into the reserved pot. Mash in the warm milk, olive oil and walnut oil; heat over low heat until warmed through. Season with about 1 teaspoon salt and a pinch of pepper.

"My kids prefer these potatoes as is, but sometimes I stir in a hint of nutmeg or lemon zest, just like my mom used to do."

rosemary-garlic potato cake

You can use a mandoline or a food processor fitted with a slicing blade to slice the potatoes superthin. To keep the potato slices from browning, put them in water and, when you're ready to assemble the dish, just drain and pat the potatoes dry.

SERVES 6 to 8   **PREP TIME** 35 minutes   **COOK TIME** 2 hours

3 large russet potatoes
(about 2 pounds/1 kg)

Extra-virgin olive oil,
for brushing (about ⅓ cup)

3 cloves garlic, finely chopped

1 teaspoon finely chopped
fresh rosemary

1 teaspoon salt

¼ teaspoon pepper

1. Preheat the oven to 425°F. Fill a large bowl with cold water. Peel the potatoes and, using a mandoline, cut the potatoes into very thin slices. Place the potatoes in the water; drain and dry well.

2. Generously grease an 8-inch (20-cm) ovenproof nonstick skillet with about 1 tablespoon olive oil. Beginning in the center, arrange the potato slices, slightly overlapping, in a circular pattern. Brush with olive oil and top with some garlic; season with some rosemary, salt and pepper. Repeat with the remaining potatoes, olive oil, garlic, rosemary, salt and pepper; press the layers down. Cover with greased foil and bake for 30 minutes. Remove the foil and continue to bake until tender and crisp, about 1½ hours. Carefully invert onto a plate; cut into wedges.

vegetables & sides

"I make this stuffing for Thanksgiving with no regrets, only thanks. I add the salty bacon for Isaiah and the sweet, tender apples for Chiara. The cornbread holds it all together in a simple dish that tastes like home."

bacon-apple cornbread stuffing

Instead of toasting the cornbread, you can spread out the pieces on a baking sheet and let them sit on your countertop overnight, uncovered, to dry out.

SERVES 6 to 8   PREP TIME 15 minutes   COOK TIME 45 minutes

2 tablespoons extra-virgin olive oil, plus more for greasing

3 slices bacon, chopped

1 small onion, chopped

2 stalks celery, thinly sliced

Salt and pepper

4 cups (1-inch/2.5-cm pieces) Double Corn Cornbread (page 75), toasted

1 Granny Smith apple—peeled, cored and finely chopped

2 teaspoons dried herb blend, such as McCormick Italian Seasoning

½ cup chopped pecans

1. Preheat the oven to 350°F. Generously grease an 8-inch (20-cm) square pan with olive oil. In a skillet, heat the olive oil over medium heat. Add the bacon and cook until the fat renders, about 3 minutes. Add the onion and celery and cook until softened, about 5 minutes; season with about ½ teaspoon salt and ¼ teaspoon pepper.

2. In a large bowl, toss together the bacon mixture, corn-bread, apple and herb blend. Transfer to the prepared pan. Scatter the pecans on top and cover with foil; bake for 15 minutes. Remove the foil; bake until crispy and golden, about 20 minutes more.

baked onions with garlic-mustard crumbs

The way the last onion layer stains the baking sheet with its caramelized sugars—that's always the best part.

SERVES 4   PREP TIME 10 minutes   COOK TIME 50 minutes

1 cup rice cereal crumbs

2 cloves garlic, grated

1½ tablespoons Dijon mustard

Salt and pepper

1 teaspoon finely chopped fresh flat-leaf parsley

1 teaspoon fresh thyme leaves, finely chopped

2 tablespoons extra-virgin olive oil, plus more for drizzling

4 large sweet onions, such as Vidalia (about 2½ pounds/ 1.25 kg), stem and root trimmed, halved crosswise

Preheat the oven to 400°F. Grease a baking sheet. In a small bowl, combine the cereal crumbs, garlic, mustard, 1 teaspoon salt, parsley, thyme and olive oil. Place the onions, cut side up, on the prepared baking sheet; season with salt and pepper and drizzle with olive oil. Top with the garlic-mustard crumbs and drizzle generously with olive oil. Cover loosely with foil; bake for 20 minutes. Remove the foil and bake until the topping is toasted and crisp, about 30 minutes more.

marshmallow-topped yam-and-chipotle bake

Purists, please leave out the chipotle pepper—a twist that adds a smoky spiciness to temper, ever so faintly, the sweetness from just about every other ingredient on the list.

SERVES 6 to 8 PREP TIME 15 minutes (plus cooling) COOK TIME 45 minutes

2 (40-ounce/1.25-kg) cans Bruce's Yams, drained

½ cup light brown sugar

1 canned chipotle chile in adobo sauce, finely chopped, or to taste

2 tablespoons extra-virgin olive oil

1 teaspoon salt

1 (20-ounce/540-mL) can crushed pineapple, drained

1 (10-ounce/300-g) bag marshmallows

Preheat the oven to 350°F. Grease a 9-inch by 13-inch (22.5-cm by 32.5-cm) baking pan. Mash together the yams, brown sugar, chipotle pepper, olive oil and salt. Stir in the pineapple; spread evenly in the prepared baking pan. Bake, stirring once, until golden and slightly dried out, 40 minutes. Top the yams with the marshmallows, pressing lightly, and bake until toasted, about 5 minutes. Let cool for 10 minutes before serving.

"This recipe belongs to my mom, who has baked these yams twice a year for nearly my entire life—at Thanksgiving and Christmas."

"This cake is my latest infatuation, with its crunchy, garlicky topping. What I love most is that it's equally delicious warm or at room temperature."

florentine cake with tomato-garlic gratin

If you prefer baking to broiling, bake the cake in a 350°F oven until set, about 10 minutes.

SERVES 6 **PREP TIME** 10 minutes **COOK TIME** 10 minutes

½ cup rice cereal crumbs

1 clove garlic, grated

½ teaspoon crushed red pepper flakes

Salt

1 tablespoon extra-virgin olive oil, plus more for drizzling

8 large eggs, at room temperature, lightly beaten

1 (10-ounce/300-g) box frozen chopped spinach, thawed and wrung dry

2 small tomatoes, sliced about ¼ inch (0.5 cm) thick

1. Preheat the broiler. In a small bowl, combine the cereal crumbs, garlic, red pepper flakes and ¼ teaspoon salt.

2. In a medium ovenproof skillet, heat the olive oil over medium-low heat. Meanwhile, in a large bowl, whisk together the eggs, spinach and 1 teaspoon salt. Pour the egg mixture into the skillet and top with the tomato slices; cook, without stirring, until set around the edges and beginning to set on top, about 4 minutes. Top with the garlic crumbs and drizzle generously with olive oil; broil until set and golden, 2 to 4 minutes.

corn pudding pie with sausage succotash

If you haven't cooked much with instant polenta, it doesn't get any easier than this recipe. Polenta is a fast, low-maintenance ingredient and perfect as a base for pudding pie.

SERVES 6 to 8   **PREP TIME** 15 minutes   **COOK TIME** 40 minutes

2 tablespoons extra-virgin olive oil, plus more for greasing

1½ pounds (750 g) fully cooked spicy Italian sausage, coarsely chopped

1 clove garlic, finely chopped

1½ cups fresh corn kernels (about 1½ ears corn) or frozen corn kernels, thawed

Salt

3 large eggs, at room temperature, separated

3 cups chicken broth

1 cup instant polenta

2 tablespoons finely chopped fresh parsley

1. Preheat the oven to 375°F. Grease a 1½-quart (1.5-L) casserole with olive oil. In a medium skillet, heat 1 tablespoon olive oil over medium-high heat and add the sausage; cook, stirring and scraping the bottom of the pan occasionally, until browned, about 5 minutes. Stir in the garlic and 1 cup corn; cook until golden, about 2 minutes, and season with ¾ teaspoon salt.

2. In a medium bowl, whisk the egg whites until soft peaks form.

3. In a medium saucepan, combine the broth, remaining 1 table-spoon olive oil and 1 teaspoon salt; bring to a boil. Reduce the heat to low and slowly stir in the polenta. Cook until thickened, stirring constantly, about 1 minute. Remove from the heat and stir in the remaining ½ cup corn. Stirring constantly, add the egg yolks, one at a time. Fold in the beaten egg whites and spread evenly in the prepared pan. Top with the sausage mixture and parsley; bake until set in the middle and golden, about 30 minutes.

"My Italian grandfather used to make a lovely sweet-and-sour carrot salad. Mine may be all sweet and no sour, but it still reminds me of him."

pumpkin pie–spiced cider-glazed roasted carrots

If there are some thick carrots in the bunch, halve them lengthwise first for even cooking.

SERVES 6   **PREP TIME** 10 minutes   **COOK TIME** 30 minutes

2 pounds (1 kg) carrots (about 12), peeled and cut diagonally into 2-inch (5-cm) pieces

2 tablespoons extra-virgin olive oil

1 cup apple cider

1 teaspoon honey

½ teaspoon pumpkin pie spice

1 teaspoon chopped fresh thyme leaves

Salt and pepper

Preheat the oven to 400°F. Place the carrots on a rimmed baking sheet. Top with the olive oil, cider, honey, pumpkin pie spice, thyme, 1 teaspoon salt and ¼ teaspoon pepper, and toss; spread out in a single layer. Roast, stirring occasionally, until the carrots are tender and the cider is syrupy, about 30 minutes.

cranberry-rosemary walnut crumble

The tart cranberries get a good dose of sweetness from the onions, balsamic vinegar and sugar, but if you want them candy-sweet, add another ¼ cup sugar.

SERVES 6   PREP TIME 15 minutes (plus resting)   COOK TIME 45 minutes

1 tablespoon extra-virgin
olive oil, plus more for
greasing and drizzling

1 medium onion, thinly sliced

¾ cup plus 1 teaspoon sugar

Salt

2 tablespoons balsamic vinegar

1 (12-ounce/375-g) bag
fresh cranberries

Finely grated zest and
juice of 1 orange

2 tablespoons Silvana's
All-Purpose Flour (page 15)

2 teaspoons finely chopped
fresh rosemary

1 cup walnuts,
coarsely chopped

½ cup rice cereal crumbs

½ teaspoon ground allspice

1. Preheat the oven to 350°F. Generously grease six 6-ounce (175-g) ovenproof glass dessert bowls or ramekins.

2. In a large skillet, heat the olive oil over medium-high heat. Add the onion, 1 teaspoon sugar and ¼ teaspoon salt and cook, stirring, until golden, about 15 minutes. Add the vinegar, stirring to loosen any brown bits on the bottom of the skillet, and cook for about 1 minute. Pour into a large bowl and add the cranberries, orange juice, flour, remaining ¾ cup sugar, 1 teaspoon rosemary and ½ cup walnuts; season with ½ teaspoon salt and toss. Transfer to the prepared bowls and bake for 15 minutes.

3. Meanwhile, in a small bowl, combine the cereal crumbs, orange zest, remaining 1 teaspoon rosemary, remaining ½ cup walnuts, allspice and ¼ teaspoon salt. Remove the bowls from the oven and top with the crumb mixture. Drizzle generously with olive oil and bake until the cranberries are tender and the crumbs are golden, about 15 minutes more. Let cool on a wire rack for about 15 minutes before serving.

"When sugar snap peas pop up at Gill's Farms near our upstate New York home, there's no stopping my kids. Just as fast as I can fill my bag, they're eating them raw by the handful."

roasted sugar snap peas

In this recipe, sugar snaps are roasted to heighten their grassy sweetness. Then they're tossed hot from the oven with lemon zest, gently lifting all of the flavors.

SERVES 4 **PREP TIME** 5 minutes **COOK TIME** 15 minutes

1 pound (500 g) sugar snap peas, trimmed

1 tablespoon extra-virgin olive oil

Salt

Finely grated zest of 1 lemon

Preheat the oven to 450°F. Place the sugar snap peas on a baking sheet and toss with the olive oil; season with about ½ teaspoon salt and spread out in a single layer. Roast, stirring once, until crisp-tender, about 15 minutes. Transfer to a medium bowl, add the lemon zest and toss.

grilled asparagus with creamy lemon dip

If you're not grilling, you can still make the dip and serve it with blanched asparagus. To blanch the asparagus, cook in salted boiling water until crisp-tender, about 3 minutes, then rinse with cold water, drain and pat dry.

SERVES 4 **PREP TIME** 15 minutes **COOK TIME** 8 minutes

2 bunches thin asparagus (about 2 pounds/1 kg), trimmed

½ cup mayonnaise, plus more for brushing

Salt and pepper

1 clove garlic, crushed

¾ teaspoon crushed red pepper flakes, or to taste

1 teaspoon apple cider vinegar or white wine vinegar

Finely grated zest and juice of 1 lemon

2 tablespoons extra-virgin olive oil

1. Preheat a grill or grill pan over medium-high heat. Brush the asparagus with mayonnaise; season with about ¼ teaspoon each salt and pepper and thread the asparagus crosswise onto the skewers. Grill, covered and turning once, until tender, 6 to 8 minutes.

2. Meanwhile, to make the dip, in a food processor, combine the mayonnaise, garlic, ½ teaspoon salt, red pepper flakes, vinegar, lemon juice and lemon zest. With the motor running, add the olive oil in a slow, steady stream and blend until smooth. Serve the dip with the grilled asparagus.

desserts

WHEN I BAKE, THERE'S COMFORT IN THE SMELL that fills the sweet, moist air—one of the reasons I once owned a bakery. I like everything about dessert—cookies and ice cream, cakes and pies. If such a trait can be inherited, Isaiah got this from me. With Chiara, signs point to no such inheritance. Maybe the daily after-school cookie routine established during Isaiah's elementary school years reinforced it. I always gave him the choice of picking out any four cookies for a snack from our local bakery. I also participated in this snack, but with just two cookies. And when it was cold outside, our cookies needed hot chocolate. Then there was the ice-cream-before-dinner habit that peaked during the summer months. My husband, Stephen, couldn't believe it when Isaiah asked him for ice cream as they walked home one evening, and he called me on the phone to confirm what he thought to be a trick Isaiah was playing on him. I then had to confess to the sugary truth. Isaiah's love of sweets couldn't all come to a crashing halt. Not if there was anything I could do about it. My persistence paid off. Now we can have our cake and eat it, too. And it tastes like cake. It looks like cake. No one ever thinks otherwise.

"Even though I try to serve—and eat—fruit for dessert, sweets just keep calling. Welcome home, dessert."

chewy chocolate chunk cookies

What's the perfect chocolate chunk cookie? The answer is in this recipe—just enough crispiness on the outside to hold the cookie together, with a chewy give on the inside. You can double the batch and save half the dough for later. Form the dough into a log and wrap it tightly in waxed paper (if the dough is too soft to handle, refrigerate first for about 30 minutes). Then refrigerate the cookie dough log until firm, about 1 hour or up to 1 week. Slice into ½-inch (1-cm) rounds and bake or freeze in a resealable plastic bag for up to 2 months. When you make the frozen cookies, add about 2 minutes to the baking time.

MAKES 18 cookies   PREP TIME 10 minutes   BAKE TIME 12 minutes

1 cup plus 3 tablespoons Silvana's All-Purpose Flour (page 15)

1 teaspoon baking powder

½ teaspoon baking soda

½ teaspoon salt

½ cup all-vegetable shortening, at room temperature

½ cup packed light brown sugar

¼ cup granulated sugar

1 large egg, at room temperature

1 teaspoon pure vanilla extract

1 cup chopped semisweet chocolate chunks

1. Preheat the oven to 375°F. Line two baking sheets with parchment paper. In a small bowl, whisk together the flour, baking powder, baking soda and salt.

2. In a large bowl and using a fork, beat together the shortening, brown sugar and granulated sugar until fluffy, about 2 minutes. Beat in the egg and vanilla. Gradually mix in the flour mixture; stir in the chopped chocolate.

3. Using a 1½-inch (3.5-cm) scoop or a rounded tablespoon, drop the dough 2 inches (5 cm) apart onto the prepared baking sheets. Bake until golden at the edges, 10 to 12 minutes. Let cool for about 2 minutes. Using a spatula, transfer to a brown paper bag–lined surface or a wire rack to cool.

VARIATION   **chewy double chocolate chunk cookies**
To make chocolate cookies, swap ¼ cup unsweetened cocoa powder for 3 tablespoons flour.

desserts

"My mom rips up brown paper shopping bags from the supermarket to use as a cooling surface for her cookies—a clever way to absorb grease."

double chocolate–cherry thumbprint cookies

These cookies are soft and melty, with just the right bit of tartness from the cherries.

MAKES 24 cookies **PREP TIME** 15 minutes (plus chilling) **COOK TIME** 12 minutes

2⅔ cups semisweet chocolate chips

2 tablespoons all-vegetable shortening, at room temperature

6 tablespoons Silvana's All-Purpose Flour (page 15)

1 teaspoon baking powder

¼ teaspoon salt

¼ cup dried cherries, chopped

2 large eggs, at room temperature

½ cup sugar

1 tablespoon pure vanilla extract

24 maraschino cherries, drained

1. Preheat the oven to 350°F. Line two baking sheets with parchment paper. In a medium microwavable bowl, melt together 1⅔ cups chocolate chips and the shortening on high heat until almost melted, about 1½ minutes; stir to combine.

2. In a small bowl, whisk together the flour, baking powder and salt; stir in the dried cherries.

3. In a large bowl, whisk together the eggs, sugar and vanilla until slightly thickened and bubbles appear. Whisk in the chocolate mixture, then gradually whisk in the flour mixture. Stir in the remaining 1 cup chocolate chips. Refrigerate until firm enough to scoop but still soft, 10 to 12 minutes. Using a 1½-inch (3.5-cm) ice cream scoop or a rounded tablespoon, drop the dough 2 inches (5 cm) apart onto the prepared baking sheets. Using your thumb or a melon baller, make an indentation in the center of each cookie; fill each with a maraschino cherry. Bake until cracks appear on the surface, about 12 minutes. Let cool on the baking sheets set on a wire rack.

"Isaiah spotted these cookies in a Brooklyn café and insisted I give them a try. I can't say I had any real motivation except to please him—and that's all it took. Now all I can say is that Isaiah was right."

lemon cream–stuffed gingerbread whoopie pies

This recipe will keep you warm—and happy—through the winter. The tart lemon cream cuts the sweet molasses ever so slightly and draws out the comforting spices.

MAKES 10 whoopie pies PREP TIME 15 minutes

6 tablespoons all-vegetable shortening, at room temperature

1½ cups confectioners' sugar, sifted

1½ tablespoons fresh lemon juice

20 Gingerbread Cookies (see below)

1. Using a handheld electric mixer, beat the shortening at medium speed until light and fluffy, about 2 minutes. Add the confectioners' sugar and mix on low speed until blended. Add the lemon juice and beat on medium-high speed until fluffy, about 2 minutes.

2. To assemble, spread the flat side of 10 cookies with the lemon cream. Top with the remaining cookies.

gingerbread cookies

MAKES 20 cookies PREP TIME 15 minutes COOK TIME 10 minutes

1½ cups Silvana's All-Purpose Flour (page 15)

2 tablespoons unsweetened cocoa powder

2 teaspoons ground ginger

1 teaspoon pumpkin pie spice

1½ teaspoons baking powder

½ teaspoon baking soda

½ teaspoon salt

½ cup vegetable oil

½ cup packed light brown sugar

3 tablespoons unsulfured molasses

1 large egg, at room temperature, lightly beaten

1. Preheat the oven to 350°F. Line two baking sheets with parchment paper. In a medium bowl, whisk together the flour, cocoa powder, ginger, pumpkin pie spice, baking powder, baking soda and salt.

2. In a large bowl, whisk together the oil and brown sugar until smooth, then whisk in the molasses and egg. Fold in the flour mixture until just combined. Using a 1½-inch (3.5-cm) ice cream scoop or a rounded tablespoon, drop mounds of batter, spaced evenly, onto the prepared baking sheets. Bake until springy to the touch, about 10 minutes. Let cool completely on the baking sheets set on a wire rack.

desserts

nut butter–and–jelly cookie cups

If you're using almond butter, stir it well before adding it to the cookie batter. You can also swap grape jelly for the strawberry.

MAKES **16 cookies** PREP TIME **25 minutes** COOK TIME **14 minutes**

½ cup Silvana's All-Purpose Flour (page 15)

1 teaspoon baking powder

¾ cup peanut butter or almond butter

¼ cup all-vegetable shortening, at room temperature

¾ cup granulated sugar

¼ teaspoon salt

1 large egg, at room temperature

Strawberry jelly, for topping

½ cup confectioners' sugar, sifted

2 tablespoons rice milk

1. Preheat the oven to 350°F. Spray two 12-cup mini muffin pans with cooking spray. In a small bowl, whisk together the flour and baking powder.

2. In a large bowl, mix together ½ cup peanut butter, the shortening, granulated sugar and salt until smooth. Beat in the egg until blended. Stir in the flour mixture until just combined. Using a 1½-inch (3.5-cm) ice cream scoop or a rounded tablespoon, drop the dough into the prepared muffin pans. Using your finger, make a small indentation in the tops. Bake until golden, 12 to 14 minutes. Let cool completely in the pan set on a wire rack.

3. Meanwhile, in a small microwavable bowl, microwave the jelly on high until runny, about 15 seconds. Spoon about ½ teaspoon jelly into the center of each cookie cup.

4. In a small bowl, beat together the remaining ¼ cup peanut butter and the confectioners' sugar; whisk in the milk. Pipe the frosting over the cookie cups in a crisscross pattern.

"These cookies are soft to the bite, slightly crumbly and greasy—yes, the good kind of greasy that you want from such a cookie."

rocky road rice crispy treats

There are rice crispy treats and then there are these. The flavors of rocky road—almonds, chocolate and marshmallow—change everything. The drizzle of melted chocolate and marshmallow sauce is just gravy.

MAKES 16 bars **PREP TIME** 5 minutes **COOK TIME** 5 minutes

4 cups mini marshmallows

½ cup well-stirred almond butter, such as Justin's Natural

¼ cup unsweetened cocoa powder

½ cup light corn syrup

½ teaspoon salt

5 cups rice cereal

¼ cup marshmallow creme, such as Fluff

2 teaspoons boiling water

¼ cup semisweet chocolate chips, melted, for drizzling

1. Grease an 8-inch (20-cm) square baking pan and line with a 14-inch (35-cm)-long piece of parchment paper, letting the ends hang over two sides of the pan. In a large saucepan, combine 2 cups marshmallows, the almond butter, cocoa powder, corn syrup and salt; cook over low heat, stirring, until melted, about 5 minutes. Stir in the cereal until almost coated, then stir in the remaining 2 cups marshmallows. Transfer to the prepared pan and, using a spatula, press evenly into the pan.

2. In a medium bowl, stir together the marshmallow creme and boiling water until smooth. Drizzle the treats with the marshmallow sauce and melted chocolate. Let cool to room temperature before cutting into squares.

"When I bake for the holidays, I want a dessert that will yield enough for seconds, and I want to be in and out of the kitchen in under an hour."

german chocolate pecan pie bars

These pecan pie bars have it all. They don't just have a classic pecan pie filling. Instead, chocolate chips are scattered over the bottom of the pie crust, and coconut is stirred in the filling for my riff on German chocolate cake.

MAKES 16 bars **PREP TIME** 20 minutes **COOK TIME** 50 minutes

½ recipe All-Purpose Pie Crust dough (page 213) or 1 pound (500 g) store-bought pie crust dough, refrigerated

½ cup semisweet chocolate chips

1 large egg, at room temperature

2 tablespoons all-vegetable shortening, at room temperature

½ teaspoon salt

¼ cup packed light brown sugar

¼ cup light corn syrup

2 cups chopped pecan halves

½ cup sweetened flake coconut

1. Preheat the oven to 400°F. On a sheet of parchment paper, roll out the dough to about ¼ inch (0.5 cm) thick. Transfer to a 9-inch (22.5-cm) square baking pan to cover the bottom, trimming any excess dough. Prick with a fork and bake until golden, 25 to 30 minutes. Scatter over the chocolate chips.

2. In a medium bowl, whisk the egg. In a heavy, medium saucepan, whisk together the shortening, salt, brown sugar and corn syrup over medium heat until melted and smooth. Whisking constantly, add to the beaten egg. Stir in the pecans and coconut; spread evenly over the crust, pressing down gently. Bake until set, about 20 minutes. Let cool completely before cutting into squares.

desserts

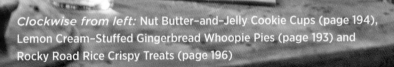

Clockwise from left: Nut Butter–and–Jelly Cookie Cups (page 194), Lemon Cream–Stuffed Gingerbread Whoopie Pies (page 193) and Rocky Road Rice Crispy Treats (page 196)

"These remind me of the brownies I grew up on—boxed mixes with the chocolate squeeze packets. Translation: Super. Fudgy. Brownies."

super fudge brownies

These brownies didn't happen overnight. The first batch was too wet. The second batch was too cakey, but the third batch was just right. You can cut, wrap and freeze these brownies, then throw them into your—or your kid's—lunchbox for a sweet treat. They'll defrost just in time for lunch.

MAKES 9 brownies PREP TIME 10 minutes COOK TIME 28 minutes

1 cup semisweet
chocolate chips, melted

¼ cup unsweetened
cocoa powder

⅓ cup vegetable oil

3 tablespoons water

1 cup sugar

2 large eggs, at room
temperature

½ cup Silvana's
All-Purpose Flour (page 15)

¼ teaspoon salt

1. Preheat the oven to 350°F. Grease an 8-inch (20-cm) square baking pan and line with a 14-inch (35-cm)-long piece of parchment paper, letting the ends hang over two sides of the pan. In a medium bowl, whisk together the melted chocolate, cocoa powder, oil and water until smooth.

2. In a large bowl, whisk together the sugar and eggs. Whisk in the chocolate mixture. Fold in the flour and salt until just combined; transfer the batter into the prepared pan and spread to the edges. Bake until set and the brownie edges pull away slightly from the sides of the pan, 25 to 28 minutes. Let cool in the pan set on a wire rack.

chocolate-covered marble loaf cake

If you're short on time, put the cake in the fridge to harden the chocolate coating.

SERVES 6 **PREP TIME** 10 minutes **COOK TIME** 50 minutes

2 tablespoons unsweetened cocoa powder

2 tablespoons boiling water

2 large eggs, at room temperature

1 cup sugar

½ cup vegetable oil

1 teaspoon pure vanilla extract

½ cup water

1 cup Silvana's All-Purpose Flour (page 15)

1 teaspoon baking powder

¼ teaspoon salt

1⅔ cups semisweet chocolate chips

3 tablespoons all-vegetable shortening, at room temperature

1. Preheat the oven to 350°F. Grease a 4½-inch by 8½-inch (11-cm by 21-cm) loaf pan. In a small bowl, whisk together the cocoa powder and boiling water.

2. In a large bowl, whisk together the eggs and sugar until pale yellow and frothy. Whisk in the oil, vanilla and water.

3. In a small bowl, whisk together the flour, baking powder and salt. Whisk into the egg mixture until just combined. Transfer one-third of the batter to a small bowl. Stir in the cocoa mixture. Alternating, spoon the vanilla and chocolate cake batters into the prepared pan. Bake until golden and a toothpick inserted in the center comes out clean, about 50 minutes. Let cool completely in the pan set on a wire rack. Remove the cake from the pan and place on the rack.

4. In a medium microwavable bowl, melt together the chocolate chips and shortening, about 1 minute; stir until smooth. Let cool slightly; using an offset spatula or the back of a spoon, coat the top and sides of the cake.

"In the summer, I like to make this upside-down cake. All I have to do is make a quick caramel, scatter over some peaches, pour the corn cake batter on top and bake."

peach-maple upside-down corn cake

When it's hot outside, you can bake this cake, covered, on the grill. If you can't find great peaches, use your favorite seasonal fruit, like cherries or plums.

SERVES 8 **PREP TIME** 20 minutes (plus cooling) **COOK TIME** 30 minutes

¾ cup sugar

1 tablespoon pure maple syrup

2 tablespoons water

2 large peaches
(about ¾ pound/375 g),
1 peeled and thinly sliced,
and 1 peeled and chopped

1 cup rice milk

1 tablespoon apple
cider vinegar

¾ cup cornmeal,
preferably medium grind

1 cup Silvana's
All-Purpose Flour (page 15)

1 tablespoon baking powder

1 teaspoon baking soda

½ teaspoon ground nutmeg

1 teaspoon salt

1 large egg, at room
temperature, lightly beaten

¼ cup vegetable oil

1. Preheat the oven to 425°F. In a 10-inch (25-cm) ovenproof skillet, combine ½ cup sugar, the maple syrup and water; bring to a boil over medium heat. Cook, without stirring, until the mixture turns a golden caramel color, about 5 minutes. Remove from the heat and place the peach slices on the bottom of the skillet.

2. In a small bowl, stir together the milk and vinegar.

3. In a medium bowl, whisk together the cornmeal, flour, remaining ¼ cup sugar, baking powder, baking soda, nutmeg and salt; stir in the chopped peaches. Add the milk mixture, egg and oil; stir until just blended. Spread the batter evenly over the sliced peaches. Bake until golden and a toothpick inserted in the center comes out clean, 20 to 25 minutes. Let cool for 15 minutes; invert onto a platter.

desserts

raspberry–lemon meringue layer cake

You can eat this cake the second you assemble the layers, or refrigerate it for at least 2 hours or up to overnight to let the flavors and textures come together.

SERVES 8 **PREP TIME** 15 minutes (plus chilling) **COOK TIME** 57 minutes (plus cooling in the oven)

meringue

6 large egg whites, at room temperature

¼ teaspoon salt

1 cup granulated sugar

1½ teaspoons cornstarch

¾ teaspoon fresh lemon juice

2 teaspoons pure vanilla extract

filling and topping

3 large eggs plus 1 large egg yolk, at room temperature

1 cup granulated sugar

½ cup fresh lemon juice

1 tablespoon finely grated lemon zest

12 ounces (340 g) raspberries

Confectioners' sugar, for sprinkling

1. Preheat the oven to 350°F. Line a baking sheet with parchment paper. Using a pencil and an 8-inch (20-cm) cake pan, outline two circles on the paper. To make the meringue layers, in the bowl of a standing mixer fitted with a whisk attachment, beat the egg whites with the salt on high speed until fluffy. Reduce the speed to medium-high and gradually beat in the granulated sugar. Beat in the cornstarch, lemon juice and vanilla until stiff and shiny. Mound half of the meringue onto each circle on the prepared baking sheet, spreading evenly to fill.

2. Reduce the oven temperature to 250°F. Bake the meringues until pale in color, about 45 minutes. Turn off the heat and let the meringue cool in the oven for 45 minutes. Remove and let cool completely on the baking sheet set on a wire rack.

3. Meanwhile, to make the filling, place a large heatproof bowl over a pot of simmering water. Add the whole eggs and egg yolk, granulated sugar, lemon juice and lemon zest; whisking constantly, cook until thickened, 10 to 12 minutes. Remove from the heat and let cool slightly. Cover the surface directly with plastic wrap; refrigerate until chilled, about 1 hour.

4. To assemble, place 1 meringue layer onto a serving plate, spread with about 1 cup lemon filling and top with half of the raspberries. Repeat with the remaining meringue layer and lemon filling. Loosely cover the cake with plastic wrap and refrigerate for at least 2 hours or overnight. To serve, top with the remaining raspberries, and using a sieve, sprinkle with confectioners' sugar.

"I wanted to make a layer cake without, well, cake. Meringue came to mind. Not the hard stuff, but the crunchy-on-the-outside and spongy-on-the-inside kind. Then I layered that with homemade lemon curd and fresh raspberries."

"If there's one dessert that I could eat every day for breakfast, lunch and dinner for the rest of my life, this is it."

chocolate birthday cake with whipped chocolate frosting

If you overwhip the chocolate frosting, just add water, a drizzle at a time, to make it glossy and smooth again.

SERVES 12   PREP TIME 30 minutes (plus cooling)   COOK TIME 30 minutes

cake

2 tablespoons instant espresso powder

1 cup boiling water

½ cup cold water

2 tablespoons pure vanilla extract

½ cup vegetable oil

2 large eggs, at room temperature

2 cups Silvana's All-Purpose Flour (page 15)

¾ cup unsweetened cocoa powder

1 cup packed light brown sugar

1 cup granulated sugar

2 teaspoons baking powder

1 teaspoon baking soda

1 teaspoon salt

frosting

3 cups semisweet chocolate chips

1½ cups water

1. Preheat the oven to 350°F. Grease two 9-inch (22.5-cm) round cake pans with cooking spray; line the bottoms with parchment paper and grease the paper. To make the cake, in a small bowl, whisk together the espresso powder and boiling water; let cool slightly. Whisk in the cold water, vanilla, oil and eggs.

2. In a large bowl, whisk together the flour, cocoa powder, brown sugar, granulated sugar, baking powder, baking soda and salt. Whisk the egg mixture into the flour mixture until just combined; divide the batter between the prepared pans. Bake until springy to the touch and a toothpick inserted in the center comes out clean, 25 to 30 minutes. Let cool completely in the pans set on a wire rack.

3. To make the frosting, in a large microwavable bowl, melt together the chocolate chips and water on high power, about 2 minutes; stir until smooth, and let cool to room temperature. With a handheld electric mixer, beat the chocolate mixture on medium-high speed until light and whipped, about 12 minutes.

4. Run a knife around the edges of the pans to release the layers. Invert one cake layer onto a cake plate, flat side facing up. Using an offset spatula or butter knife, spread about 2 cups of the whipped chocolate frosting evenly on top. Invert the remaining cake layer, rounded side up, onto the frosting. Frost the top and sides of the cake with the remaining frosting. Refrigerate for about 30 minutes before slicing.

strawberry cupcakes with strawberry frosting

These moist, tender cupcakes have a nice strawberry flavor without being too sweet. The strawberry frosting is wonderfully lush and creamy.

MAKES 12 cupcakes **PREP TIME** 18 minutes **COOK TIME** 20 minutes

cupcakes

1½ cups Silvana's All-Purpose Flour (page 15)

2 teaspoons baking powder

½ teaspoon salt

½ cup strawberry puree (about 5 ounces/150 g strawberries)

½ cup rice milk

2 teaspoons pure vanilla extract

3 drops red food coloring

½ cup all-vegetable shortening, at room temperature

1 cup granulated sugar

2 large eggs, at room temperature

frosting

1 cup all-vegetable shortening, at room temperature

2¾ cups confectioners' sugar, sifted

½ cup strawberry puree (about 5 ounces/150 g strawberries)

¼ teaspoon salt

Pink sprinkles, for topping

1. Preheat the oven to 350°F. Line a 12-cup muffin pan with paper liners. To make the cupcakes, in a small bowl, whisk together the flour, baking powder and salt.

2. In another small bowl, combine the strawberry puree, milk, vanilla and food coloring.

3. In a large bowl and using a handheld electric mixer, beat the shortening on medium-high speed until fluffy, about 1 minute. Add the granulated sugar and beat until fluffy, about 2 minutes. On medium speed, beat in the eggs, one at a time, until combined. Alternately add the flour mixture and the strawberry mixture, beginning and ending with the flour mixture and beating until just combined. Pour the batter into the prepared muffin pan until each cup is two-thirds full. Bake until the cupcakes are springy to the touch and a toothpick inserted in the center comes out clean, 18 to 20 minutes. Let cool completely in the pan set on a wire rack.

4. To make the frosting, in a large bowl and using a handheld electric mixer, beat together the shortening, confectioners' sugar, strawberry puree and salt on medium-high speed until fluffy. Pipe or spread over the cooled cupcakes; top with sprinkles.

toasted marshmallow–topped pumpkin ice cream pie with a gingerbread cookie crust

The vanilla bean lends a toasty caramelized flavor, plus you get beautifully speckled ice cream. Also, you can rinse the vanilla bean with water after using, let it dry and bury it in granulated sugar for extra flavor.

SERVES 8 PREP TIME 35 minutes (plus cooling and freezing) COOK TIME 30 minutes

ice cream

1½ cups rice milk

3 tablespoons cornstarch

3 large eggs plus 2 large egg yolks, at room temperature

½ cup packed light brown sugar

1 vanilla bean, split lengthwise, or 1 teaspoon pure vanilla extract

⅛ teaspoon ground cinnamon

⅛ teaspoon salt

⅓ cup canned pure pumpkin puree

crust and topping

1½ cups cookie crumbs from homemade (page 193) or store-bought gingerbread cookies (about 7 cookies)

5 tablespoons all-vegetable shortening, melted

1 large egg white, at room temperature

3 cups mini marshmallows

1. In a small bowl, stir together ½ cup milk with the cornstarch.

2. Place a large heatproof bowl over a pot of simmering water. Add the whole eggs, egg yolks, brown sugar, vanilla bean, cinnamon, salt and remaining 1 cup milk; whisking constantly, cook until steaming, about 5 minutes. Whisk in the cornstarch mixture and cook, whisking constantly, until thickened, 6 to 8 minutes more. Remove from the heat and stir in the pumpkin puree. Let cool slightly. Cover the surface directly with plastic wrap and refrigerate until cold, at least 2 hours.

3. Meanwhile, to make the crust, in a small bowl, combine the cookie crumbs and shortening. Press the mixture onto the bottom and up the sides of a 9-inch (22.5-cm) pie plate; freeze until set, about 20 minutes.

4. Preheat the oven to 350°. In a small bowl, beat the egg white with a fork and lightly brush on the pie shell. Bake for 15 minutes. Let cool completely.

5. Remove the vanilla bean from the cold pumpkin custard and pour into an ice cream machine; process until the consistency of soft-serve ice cream, 20 to 25 minutes. Transfer the ice cream into the cooled cookie crust, spreading evenly. Freeze until firm, about 4 hours.

6. Preheat the broiler. Top the pie with the marshmallows and broil until lightly browned, 1 to 2 minutes.

desserts

chocolate mousse cloud pie with a chocolate cookie crust

Smooth. Silky. Chocolaty. This mousse is mesmerizing. All you really need is a spoon. But it only gets better served in a chocolate cookie crust and topped with chocolate shavings.

SERVES 8 PREP TIME 20 minutes (plus chilling and freezing) COOK TIME 5 minutes

1½ cups cookie crumbs from homemade (page 190) or store-bought chocolate cookies (about 7 cookies)

5 tablespoons all-vegetable shortening, melted

6 large eggs, separated, plus 1 large egg white, at room temperature

2 tablespoons sugar

10 ounces (300 g) semisweet chocolate, coarsely chopped, plus more for shaving

½ teaspoon salt

½ teaspoon cream of tartar

1. In a small bowl, combine the cookie crumbs and shortening. Press the mixture onto the bottom and up the sides of a 9-inch (22.5-cm) pie plate; freeze until set, about 20 minutes.

2. Preheat the oven to 350°F. In a small bowl, beat the 1 egg white with a fork and lightly brush on the pie shell. Bake for 15 minutes. Let cool completely.

3. Meanwhile, place a medium heatproof bowl over a pot of simmering water. Add the 6 egg yolks and 1 tablespoon sugar and whisk until pale yellow and thickened, about 3 minutes. Remove from the heat.

4. Place a separate medium heatproof bowl over a pot of simmering water. Add the chocolate and stir until melted. Let cool slightly, then whisk into the beaten yolks.

5. In a large heatproof bowl, whisk together the remaining 6 egg whites, remaining 1 tablespoon sugar, salt and cream of tartar until combined. Place over a pot of barely simmering water and cook, whisking, until the sugar dissolves and the mixture is hot to the touch, 2 to 3 minutes. Remove from the heat and, using a handheld electric mixer, beat on high speed until stiff, glossy peaks form and the mixture is cooled, 7 to 10 minutes. Fold half of the egg white mixture into the chocolate mixture, then fold in the remaining egg white mixture until just smooth. Gently transfer the mousse into the cooled cookie crust. Refrigerate until set, at least 3 hours. Before serving, top with chocolate shavings.

desserts

double-crusted double apple pie

The "double" in this pie is not just the crust, but the apple. Along with the Granny Smith apples, I like to use apple butter—really just concentrated applesauce—which adds an unexpected depth of flavor. You can find it in the jam and jelly aisle of your local supermarket.

SERVES 8   PREP TIME 25 minutes   COOK TIME 1 hour 15 minutes

6 Granny Smith apples
(about 2½ pounds/1.25 kg)—
peeled, cored and sliced ¼ inch
(0.5 cm) thick

1 tablespoon fresh lemon juice

¾ cup packed light
brown sugar

2 tablespoons Silvana's
All-Purpose Flour (page 15)

1¾ pounds (875 g)
All-Purpose Pie Crust dough
(opposite page) or about
2 pounds (1 kg) store-bought
pie crust dough, refrigerated

¼ cup apple butter

1 large egg, at room
temperature

1 teaspoon water

1. Place a rack in the lower third of the oven and preheat to 400°F. In a large bowl, toss together the apples, lemon juice, ½ cup brown sugar and flour.

2. On a piece of parchment paper, roll out each dough disk until about 11 inches (27.5 cm) in diameter and about ¼ inch (0.5 cm) thick. Line a 9-inch (22.5-cm) metal pie plate with one dough round to cover the bottom and sides. Spread the apple butter on the bottom and top with the apple mixture; cover with the remaining dough round, crimp the edges to seal and cut a few slits on top.

3. In a small bowl, beat together the egg, remaining ¼ cup brown sugar and water. Place the pie on a baking sheet and brush with the egg mixture. Bake for 40 minutes. Lower the oven temperature to 350°F and bake until golden, about 35 minutes more. Let cool on a wire rack.

all-purpose pie crust

This crust is a small, flaky miracle. The pie crust dough and baked, cooled pie crusts will keep, covered, for up to 2 days in the fridge or up to 3 months in the freezer. To prevent the edges from overbrowning when baking, loosely cover them with aluminum foil. You can make an adjustable foil ring: Take a 10-inch (25-cm)-square piece of heavy-duty aluminum foil and fold in four, then cut out a quarter-circle, leaving about a 2-inch (5-cm) perimeter. For the most even browning, bake the pie crusts separately. If you're short on time, stagger both pie crusts on the same oven rack. Halfway through baking, switch positions and rotate each pie crust a half-turn.

MAKES Two 9-inch (22.5-cm) pie shells, or about 1¾ pounds (875 g) pie crust dough
PREP TIME 25 minutes (plus freezing) COOK TIME 40 minutes

2¾ cups Silvana's All-Purpose Flour (page 15), plus more for dusting

½ teaspoon salt

1⅓ cups chilled all-vegetable shortening, cut into small pieces

⅔ cup ice water

1. In a food processor, pulse together the flour and salt. Add the shortening and pulse until coarse crumbs form, about 10 seconds. Pour in the ice water and pulse until the dough comes together and the water is fully incorporated, about 30 seconds. Divide into two equal pieces, wrap each in plastic wrap and flatten each into a disk. Freeze until firm, about 15 minutes.

2. Position a rack in the middle of the oven and preheat to 400°F. On a lightly floured work surface, roll out 1 pie crust dough until about 11 inches (27.5 cm) in diameter and about ¼ inch (0.5 cm) thick. Line a 9-inch (22.5-cm) metal pie plate with the dough to cover the bottom and sides; crimp the edges and prick with a fork. Bake for 30 minutes; cover the edges with foil. Continue to bake until golden, about 10 minutes more. Let cool completely on a wire rack. Repeat with the remaining pie crust dough.

"I couldn't resist coating the insides of the waffle cones with chocolate and leaving a last-bite surprise in the bottom."

strawberry swirl ice cream with chocolate-dipped waffle cones

If you're looking for a shortcut, buy strawberry sorbet. Or, you can freeze the ice cream while you make the waffle cones.

SERVES 6 PREP TIME 30 minutes (plus cooling and freezing) COOK TIME 43 minutes

3 cups fresh strawberries (about 1 pound/500 g), hulled and finely chopped

¾ cup sugar

1½ cups rice milk

3 tablespoons cornstarch

3 large eggs plus 2 large egg yolks, at room temperature

⅛ teaspoon salt

6 Chocolate-Dipped Waffle Cones (page 216)

1. In a small saucepan, combine the strawberries and ¼ cup sugar. Bring to a simmer over medium heat, stirring and mashing occasionally; cook until bubbling and jamlike, about 30 minutes (you should have 1 cup).

2. Meanwhile, in a small bowl, stir together ½ cup milk with the cornstarch.

3. Place a large heatproof bowl over a pot of simmering water. Add the whole eggs, egg yolks, remaining ½ cup sugar, remaining 1 cup milk and salt; whisking constantly, cook until steaming, about 5 minutes. Whisk in the cornstarch mixture and cook, whisking constantly, until thickened, about 8 minutes. Remove from the heat and stir in ½ cup cooked strawberries. Let cool slightly. Cover the surface directly with plastic wrap and refrigerate until cold, at least 2 hours.

4. Using a sieve, strain the custard, pressing down with a rubber spatula. Pour into an ice cream machine and process until the consistency of soft-serve ice cream, 20 to 25 minutes. With the motor running, stream in the remaining cooked strawberries to swirl. Transfer to an airtight container and freeze until firm, at least 4 hours. To serve, scoop the ice cream into the waffle cones.

chocolate-dipped waffle cones

If you don't already have a waffle cone machine, it's a small investment with almost instant gratification. The second you breathe in that one and only sweet smell of waffles cooking, you'll know that you made the right decision. You can make extra waffle cones and store them in a resealable plastic bag for later. If you want to make chocolate waffle cones, just substitute ¼ cup unsweetened cocoa powder for ¼ cup flour.

MAKES 15 waffle cones   PREP TIME 10 minutes   COOK TIME 17 minutes

1¾ cups Silvana's
All-Purpose Flour (page 15)

2 teaspoons baking powder

½ teaspoon ground cinnamon

3 large eggs

¾ cup sugar

½ cup plus 2 tablespoons
vegetable oil

1 teaspoon pure vanilla extract

1 pound (500 g) chocolate,
coarsely chopped

Rainbow sprinkles,
for decorating

1. In a small bowl, whisk together the flour, baking powder and cinnamon. In a medium bowl, whisk together the eggs and sugar until pale yellow and frothy. Stir in ½ cup oil and the vanilla, then fold in the flour mixture until just combined.

2. Preheat a waffle cone machine to darkness level 4. Grease with nonstick cooking spray. Spoon 2 tablespoons batter into the center and close; bake until golden, about 1 minute. Working quickly, roll the waffle around a cone form, sealing the tip and holding in place for a few seconds to set. Let cool on a wire rack. Repeat with the remaining batter.

3. In a small bowl, microwave the chocolate and the remaining 2 tablespoons oil at high power, stirring every 30 seconds, until smooth, 1 to 2 minutes. Place a wire rack over a sheet of waxed paper. Working one at a time and using a brush, spread a thin coat of the melted chocolate mixture on the inside of the cone. Dip the cone into the melted chocolate mixture, forming a band around the top, and decorate with sprinkles. Fill the inside tip with about 1 inch (2.5 cm) of melted chocolate mixture and set on the wire rack. Repeat with the remaining waffle cones.

brown sugar–pecan ice cream snickerdoodle sandwiches

MAKES 8 ice cream sandwiches PREP TIME 45 minutes (plus chilling and freezing) COOK TIME 25 minutes

ice cream

1½ cups rice milk

3 tablespoons cornstarch

3 large eggs plus 2 large egg yolks, at room temperature

1 cup pecans, ½ cup finely crushed and ½ cup coarsely chopped

½ cup packed light brown sugar

⅛ teaspoon salt

⅛ teaspoon ground cinnamon

cookies

1 cup plus 3 tablespoons Silvana's All-Purpose Flour (page 15)

1 teaspoon baking powder

½ teaspoon baking soda

½ teaspoon salt

⅛ plus ½ teaspoon ground cinnamon

½ cup all-vegetable shortening, at room temperature

½ cup packed light brown sugar

6 tablespoons granulated sugar

1 large egg, at room temperature

1 teaspoon pure vanilla extract

1. To make the ice cream, in a small bowl, stir together ½ cup milk and the cornstarch.

2. Place a large heatproof bowl over a pot of simmering water. Add the whole eggs, egg yolks, finely crushed pecans, brown sugar, salt, cinnamon and remaining 1 cup milk; whisking constantly, cook until steaming, about 5 minutes. Whisk in the cornstarch mixture and cook, whisking constantly, until thickened, 6 to 8 minutes more. Let cool slightly. Cover the surface directly with plastic wrap and refrigerate until cold, at least 2 hours.

3. Strain the custard, pressing down with a rubber spatula. Pour into an ice cream machine and process until the consistency of soft-serve ice cream, 20 to 25 minutes. Stir in the coarsely chopped pecans. Transfer to an airtight container and freeze until firm, at least 4 hours.

4. Meanwhile, preheat the oven to 375°F. Line two baking sheets with parchment paper. To make the cookies, in a small bowl, whisk together the flour, baking powder, baking soda, salt and ⅛ teaspoon cinnamon.

5. In a large bowl and using a fork, beat together the shortening, brown sugar and 4 tablespoons granulated sugar until fluffy, about 2 minutes. Beat in the egg and vanilla. Gradually beat in the flour mixture.

6. In a small bowl, mix together the remaining 2 tablespoons granulated sugar and remaining ½ teaspoon cinnamon. Using a 1½-inch (3.5-cm) ice cream scoop, scoop up rounds of dough and dip the rounded side of the dough into the cinnamon-sugar mixture to coat; place 2 inches (5 cm) apart sugared side up on the prepared baking sheets and bake until golden at the edges, about 10 minutes. Let cool for about 2 minutes. Using a spatula, transfer to a wire rack to cool completely.

7. To assemble, sandwich about 2 tablespoons or two 1½-inch (3.5-cm) scoops slightly softened ice cream between two cookies, pressing down gently. Working quickly, repeat with the remaining ice cream and cookies. Freeze until firm, about 30 minutes. To serve, let soften in the refrigerator for about 10 minutes or microwave for 20 seconds.

desserts

"I've eaten enough caramel corn to last a lifetime—starting with Cracker Jacks and working my way up to the fancy brands. Who knew it was so easy to make?"

caramel corn chocolate-pecan bark

A little kosher salt—available at your supermarket—makes a big difference in this recipe.

SERVES 8 **PREP TIME** 5 minutes **COOK TIME** 20 minutes

1 cup sugar

2 tablespoons light corn syrup

2 tablespoons water

6 cups freshly popped or store-bought unsalted popcorn

1 cup chopped roasted salted pecans

1⅔ cups semisweet chocolate chips, melted

Salt, preferably kosher, for sprinkling (optional)

1. Line a rimmed baking sheet with parchment paper. In a medium saucepan, combine the sugar, corn syrup and water; bring to a boil over medium heat. Cook, without stirring, until a golden caramel color forms, about 20 minutes; remove from the heat.

2. Working quickly, stir in the popcorn, then transfer the caramel corn to the prepared baking sheet and spread out in an even layer. Top with the pecans and pour the melted chocolate chips on top, spreading to cover; sprinkle with salt, if using. Let cool completely, then cut into clusters.

index

NOTE: Page references in *italics* indicate photographs.

index

222

acknowledgments

I give my love to my family, who hold my heart. To my ever-loving husband, Stephen, who photographed each stunning image in this cookbook and beyond. I would not be me without you. To my angel face, Isaiah, for whom I wrote each and every word on these pages. You are always on my mind. And to my sweet, sweet Chiara, who shines so bright with each smile. No one makes me laugh as much as you. To my mom, Penny Nardone, and dad, Silverio Nardone, who taught me how to see the world through food—an indescribable and sometimes humbling truth. To my brother, Bernardo, who holds his own in the kitchen but every now and then lets his little sister make him a home-cooked meal. And to my mother-in-law, Marcia Gross, for her endless emotional encouragement.

To Rachael Ray and John Cusimano, for years of good food and great friendship. To my *Every Day with Rachael Ray* magazine staff for their everlasting support and inspiration. To my agent, Doe Coover, who turned a whisper of a conversation into an incredible cookbook deal. To the entire Reader's Digest team, especially Harold Clarke, Dolores York, Stacey Ashton and George McKeon, all who helped realize my vision for the project every step of the way and let me be myself. To Tracey Seaman, my close friend of more than 16 years, who made my food look every bit delicious. To Alison Lew, who made Isaiah and my story come to life through her fearless design, and to Timothy Michael Cooper, Andrea Chesman and Barbara Booth, who kept all things consistent. To my recipe testers, Mian Catalano and Monica Hutchinson, who made absolutely sure that each recipe works. To my photography crew—Elizabeth Tunnicliffe, Meghan Guthrie, Djordje Skendzic and Vanessa Boer—together with Stephen: All of you defined the images with your talented eyes. To my friend and colleague, Barbara Kempe, for all of the little favors. To Dr. Donielle Wilson, who transformed our lives for the better. To Christina Stanley-Salerno, Anne Harmon and Allyson Fisher, my friends for life, who kept me on track. A huge thanks to Kiplyn Kirby for always taking great care of us. And here's to everyone who has shaped my destiny through to today.

table of equivalents

volume

IMPERIAL	METRIC
⅛ teaspoon	0.5 mL
¼ teaspoon	1 mL
½ teaspoon	2 mL
¾ teaspoon	4 mL
1 teaspoon	5 mL
1 tablespoon	15 mL
¼ cup	50 mL
⅓ cup	75 mL
½ cup	125 mL
⅔ cup	150 mL
¾ cup	175 mL
1 cup	250 mL

weight

IMPERIAL	METRIC
¼ ounce	7.5 g
½ ounce	15 g
¾ ounce	20 g
1 ounce	30 g
8 ounces (½ pound)	250 g
16 ounces (1 pound)	500 g
32 ounces (2 pounds)	1 kg

NOTE: *Equivalents have been rounded for convenience.*

temperature

IMPERIAL	METRIC
300°F	150°C
325°F	160°C
350°F	180°C
375°F	190°C
400°F	200°C
425°F	220°C

length

IMPERIAL	METRIC
⅛ inch	3 mm
¼ inch	6 mm
½ inch	1 cm
1 inch	2.5 cm